Trauma Magic

Clementine Morrigan

Trauma Magic

By Clementine Morrigan

Published by Clementine Morrigan
Montreal, Quebec

Clementinemorrigan.com

ISBN 978-1-9881780-1-1

Layout design by Madeline Stocking

Cover art by Dev Murphy

Cover design by Jay Marquis-Manicom

Also by
Clementine Morrigan

Rupture (2012)

You Can't Own the Fucking Stars (2018)

Sexting (2021)

Fucking Magic (2021)

Table of Contents

For Cressida. I remember you.

Foreward

Years ago, hip-deep in swamp water, I came to the conclusion that I may be too broken to survive on this planet.

The struggles inherent with the project in which I was enmeshed—professional treeplanting in Canada's northern boreal forests—was honestly just the catalyst for this particularly depressing thought. The paradigm that held it was one which considers trauma a handicap, and not a rich site of possibility. While my body was being worn away by work, I was being made aware of just how busted up I already was on the inside. Later, my doctors would click their tongues at my scar tissue. Call them micro-tears. Lesions. Repetitive motion, you know. All those small traumas, they add up.

Clementine Morrigan's work joins a chorus of other disabled writers who are calling us to consider what non-normative bodies and minds have to celebrate—Morrigan asks us in *Trauma as Possibility* to pick apart violence and its effects: to value the traumatized experience while we continue to resist and oppose the violence which originates it. Upon my first reading of this text, I was undone. This is what my advocates, my therapists, *my true friends* have been saying all along: that my body, bodies like mine, minds like mine—they are not fractured, mortally wounded, *fucked up beyond all recognition*. If a normative understanding of good bodies and good minds does not have space for us, we must change our understanding of what it is to be good—better yet, destroy the binary of good and bad altogether, when it comes to what simply is. Beginning in my body, I accept what it is, because it is what it is. I accept who I love, because they are who I love. I accept the world, because I know it is good enough, because it has to be. Because it is the one I have. I pull myself out of the swamp, which is not my enemy. I will not die here.

Trauma Magic originally appeared in zine format. As an editor, I have helped Clementine move their many citations from in-text MLA to footnote Chicago, for ease of reading. I have made suggestions for expansion, which Clementine has taken. Most notably, I have arranged the text into the narrative I saw: a hero's journey. From a real world full of enchantment and love, our protagonist sets out with her spirit guides (the fairies enchanting the lakes, hills and fields of Ontario. The distant call of the old Irish gods. Creator, as manifested through the animals and plants and the sacred relations of each and every living thing. Holy Mary, Mother of God. Sweet Mary, lost little girl. Mighty Mary, queen of the world) through a dark underbelly of physical and chemical incarceration, ruled over by the comforting lies and false idols of addiction and capital, to return home—which is enchanted, as it should be—to the innocence of friendship, and love, and pleasure.

I couldn't be happier to introduce this book to you, by Clementine Morrigan, who is a writer, and a sage, and an unburnt witch. I am happy to call them my comrade, my colleague, and my friend.

Tara McGowan-Ross, editor
Montreal
Plague Winter
2020

Be Changed:
An
Introduction

Trauma Magic came into being as my Masters thesis in the field of Environmental Studies. I wrote the first versions of these essays sometime between 2015 and 2017, except for "Fucking Crazy," which was added later. These essays were my desperate and driven attempt to find and love my crazy hurting self, to declare with courage and conviction that my life is not a waste or a tragedy. They were a quest to find and remember magic, to dare to bring magic into the cold, disenchanted university. The writing itself was magic, a synthesis, a ritual, a pulling together of disparate threads.

It's hard being crazy in grad school. I'm lucky I was in a program that gave me a lot of leeway to be weird. I'm lucky that I was able to access financial support from the government for my complex ptsd (school would not have been possible for me otherwise). I'm lucky that I was able to register for disability services and get my access needs met, which mainly meant being allowed to hand things in late. I was lucky to be sober and alive and in grad school trying to make sense out of everything. These essays were the result of a long journey and a lot of prior struggle, as well as the luck of living where there was enough of a welfare state and the luck of being able to find good enough therapy. They are a testament to a huge amount of healing work already done.

But I want to be honest with you, I was in so much pain when I wrote these essays, and that pain has changed and transformed in many ways since writing them. I think that transformation is visible when transitioning into the final essay "Fucking Crazy", which I decided to add because of how much it resonates with and extends the earlier work. One thing I want to be very upfront about here in this introduction is that when I wrote these essays, I did not have access to the knowledge systems or therapeutic modalities which have most helped me live my best life as a crazy and traumatized person. This is because accurate information about complex trauma is hard to come by, and, crucially, access to effective trauma treatment is wildly inaccessible for most people.

The therapist who told me complex ptsd is permanent and that I should expect to live with it for the rest of my life was doing talk therapy with me. Talk therapy on its own is not an effective treatment for complex ptsd. Since learning attachment theory, polyvagal theory, and the theory of structural dissociation, and working with a therapist who understands complex trauma and structural dissociation, I have come so far. I still have complex ptsd and it is true that I will never be like someone who has not had the life that I had, but I have also found that a massive amount of healing and transformation is possible, and I am grateful for that healing and transformation, even as I love everything I have learned from my trauma.

I have changed and healed so much since writing this book. I am, in many very real ways, not the same person you will find in these pages. The thing about trauma magic is that it changes you. Far from being a static state, it is a dynamic living process. When I am connected to the practice of magic and the work of healing and loving my trauma, I go through regular profound transformations. I have recently completed yet another one. And, it is the girl in these pages, her love of magic, and her astounding courage that got me to where I am today. This work was an important part of my process, an important part of my journey to loving myself completely, and living a full and beautiful life.

In 2019, I edited down my Masters thesis to a few select essays, the ones that held the most power, truth, and magic, and compiled them into a zine titled *Trauma Magic*, adding the essay "Fucking Crazy" which was written some time in 2018. This project existed in that incarnation for a couple of years. In 2020 I submitted the zine to a press and got a book deal. I was lucky enough to work with Tara McGowan-Ross, a cherished friend and comrade, and one of my favourite poets, as an editor. Tara read the manuscript and completely reimagined it, making major suggestions for a creative restructuring of the work. I worked closely with her edits because I respect her brilliant mind. What you see here is the result.

The press which picked up the book ended up dissolving before the publication happened. And so, I decided to embrace my roots as an independent writer, zinester, and punk, and publish the work myself. I am also facing the reality that publishing with presses is no longer a likely trajectory for me, because I have been heavily targeted by cancel culture. (That is a another story, one related to my increasing recovery from trauma resulting in no longer having a fawn response, and one you can hear about on my podcast *Fucking Cancelled* if you are interested).

I have changed so profoundly since writing these words. I made edits where possible to bring this work into closer alignment with where I am today, while trying to strike a balance with my past self. I am happy with the outcome. It was beautiful time travel to retrace the trajectories in this book, to revisit the various incarnations of myself in these pages, with all the wisdom they have to offer the person I am now, and all the wisdom I have to offer them. If you are interested in where I have gone and how I have changed since, you can find more of my writing projects on my website, clementinemorrigan.com.

I offer this book to you now as a prayer. It is a prayer for a way back, back to the power and the magic and the truth. It is a seeking of enchantment and relationship and responsibility. It is love, in all its transformative potential, love that does not look away, that is not earned, but is given freely to all. It is an invitation to love yourself as you are. It is an invitation to turn toward the world and be changed by it.

Whoever you are and wherever you are on your own path, I'm grateful you found your way here. Thank you for being on this journey with me.

Clementine Morrigan
Montreal
Plague Spring
2021

Trauma

as

Possibility

This book is about trauma.

Before beginning I will take some time to unpack what I mean when I use the word 'trauma' and how I intend to make use of the term. I define trauma as an ongoing, embodied way of being, resulting from traumatic experiences – often, though not exclusively, of violence. I use 'trauma' rather than post-traumatic stress disorder (hereafter referred to as ptsd), or other diagnostic labels, as a way to name an ongoing, embodied experience of disability, without relying on psychiatric language which can be alienating, or inaccessible to many people.

I understand trauma as an emotional, mental, physiological, and physical disability which can result from traumatic experiences. I recognize that not everyone's trauma is validated as disability, because the normalization of violence toward working class, racialized, Indigenous, and Third World people can work to frame the resulting trauma as unremarkable, unimportant, or as a 'natural' state.[1] [2]

I also acknowledge that discourses of trauma can be mobilized in harmful ways: by framing trauma as a personal dysfunction rather than a response to systemic violence, by locating violence in the past rather than naming violence as ongoing, and by framing people, and populations, who live with trauma as overcome by trauma and therefore unable to make decisions for themselves. Dian Million in *Therapeutic Nations: Healing in an Age of Indigenous Human Rights*, explains that trauma can be deployed in service of neoliberalism by focusing on individual healing rather than systemic justice, and that discourses of trauma are utilized by colonial nation-states to distract from, and deny, the importance of Indigenous sovereignty.[3] Million visions a healing that is firmly rooted in justice, rather than state-sanctioned attempts at healing which ignore the reality of ongoing violence.[4]

---

[1] Erevelles, *Disability and difference in global contexts.*

[2] Mbembe, "Necropolitics."

[3] Million, *Therapeutic nations.*

[4] ibid

Despite the harmful ways which trauma can be mobilized, I remain committed to trauma as an analytic. It is necessary to have language to discuss not only violence, but the ongoing emotional, mental, physiological, and physical disablement produced through violence. When discussions focus only on violence, and reject naming the ongoing and embodied experiences which can result from that violence, much is lost. I am particularly concerned about trauma being reduced to the violence which originates it, because I understand trauma not as a tragedy, but as a strategy of survival and resistance. While using the word 'trauma', it is important to remain critical of the ways that this term can be deployed to psychiatrize, dismiss, or ignore survivors of violence, or to validate the trauma of some violences and not others. With this in mind, I suggest that there are ways to make use of the concept of 'trauma' which foreground liberation. An important part of this is valuing experiences of trauma, even as we resist violence which traumatizes.

Trauma is the body saying no. Trauma makes visible what we are forbidden to speak. Trauma is the drive toward life and toward escape. It is the smoke that lets us know the house is on fire. It is a massively creative attempt to bear the unbearable, to make meaning out of the unthinkable. It is the ushering of whatever power and resistance is available, even if the scope of that power and resistance lies only within the body. It is a desperate attempt to live, even when that looks like an attempt at dying. While trauma is pathologized and seen as sickness, I understand trauma as a natural and ingenious response to circumstances which terrify and overwhelm beyond measure. When we understand trauma only as the violence which precedes it, we miss the brilliant ways that people manage to survive—and, sometimes, to escape and transform.

Within critical disability studies, there has been a move toward desiring disability. Ableist framings of disability have long constructed disability as something tragic and unwanted, something to be moved away from at all costs. Disability scholars, artists, and activists challenge this framing by highlighting what is delicious and desirable about disabled experience.

Mia Mingus states, "we must move toward the ugly. Not just the ugly in ourselves, but the people and communities that are ugly, undesirable, unwanted, disposable, hidden, displaced."[5] What shifts inside of us when we move toward the ugly, the rejected, the unwanted, and the unloved? What becomes possible in our communities when we value ugliness? Edward Ndopu writes, "disability is an offering to humanity that enables us as individuals to divest from that suffocating thing we call 'normal.'"[6] Are we even aware of the way 'normal' suffocates us? What boundless freedoms might lie on the other side of normal? Robert McRuer asks, "what might it mean to welcome the disability to come, to desire it? What might it mean to shape worlds capable of welcoming the disability to come?"[7] What would happen if we could be curious about the changes that come as we age, as we experience injuries and illness? What would become possible when disability is framed as possibility rather than only as loss?

Resisting ableist framings of disability as a condition in need of a cure, or as a state of perpetual lack, disability theorists have suggested that disability is desirable. Disabled embodiments are ways of being in the world, which offer their own possibilities. Compassion, curiosity, even excitement and desire are extended to experiences which are rejected by an ableist culture. Yet, even within critical disability scholarship, this important reframing of disability is not usually extended to experiences of trauma. Trauma remains framed as a negative, a tragedy, and something to be moved away from at all costs. It is bound up with its origins, usually violence, and therefore seen as irredeemable.

---

[5] Mingus, "Moving toward the ugly."

[6] Ndopu, "Don't deny me my disability, dignity, and equal opportunity."

[7] McRuer, *Crip theory*.

Since violence is not celebrated or desired within movements for social justice, trauma is also not celebrated or desired. For those of us who are traumatized, indefinitely and perhaps permanently disabled by trauma, this view of trauma is constricting. It condemns us to a relationship with our embodied experiences which is fundamentally grounded in rejection. It is possible, instead, to hold the complexity of resisting violence, while loving and valuing the embodied experience of traumatized people.

My hope is to reframe trauma, to reimagine it as a site of possibility. I argue that embodied experiences of trauma are one means with which to resist violence, and that embodied experiences of trauma can offer new ways of being in the world. I draw upon the work of critical disability and disability justice thinkers, as well as my own lived experience as a traumatized person in order to make this argument. I consider trauma in relation to queer temporalities. I consider trauma in relation to the complex, multispecies, ecological world we live in. I consider trauma in relation to magic. By staying with trauma and engaging it as a strategy of resistance and a site of possibility, I insist on the simultaneous importance of working to end violence, and desiring the difference of the disabled embodiment that is trauma.

Rather than understand trauma as a passive response to violence, I frame trauma as an active strategy of resistance. Trauma can be disruptive and interrupt the flow of business as usual. Self-injury, addiction, eating disorders, suicide attempts, and other behaviors associated with trauma act as red flags indicating that something is very wrong. While medical and psychiatric discourses work hard to locate the cause of these behaviours in personal dysfunction, the behaviours themselves frequently lead back to violence. Patty Berne writes, "we know that we are powerful not despite the complexities of our bodies, but because of them."[8] The behaviours associated with trauma, so often framed as pathological and negative, can be understood as powerful

---

[8] Berne, "Disability justice – a working draft."

acts of resistance against violence. The experience of violence can be one of complete powerlessness, in which every attempt to fight or flee has been thwarted. In most cases, the violence continues, because it is systemic, and because it remains unaddressed. Since fighting and fleeing have not prevented the violence, trauma takes over as a strategy of resistance. Trauma can make it very difficult to pretend that nothing is happening.

As a child, I experienced sexual abuse at the hands of my grandfather. Running from and resisting him resulted in punishment, so I learned to submit. None of the adults in my life protected me or intervened. I began cutting myself and overdosing on Tylenol. I did this because I was in a great deal of pain. Yet, these actions were also resistance. Within the space of my family, I was expected to act as if nothing was wrong. While I learned to submit to my grandfather and be 'good,' my cutting and overdosing made visible that the situation I was in was not okay. I was forced to see a social worker at my school and ended up disclosing what was happening to me. This resulted in me never having to see my grandfather again.

While I did experience psychiatric incarceration and further violence due to my trauma-based behaviours, I was still successful in removing myself from the primary source of abuse in my life. Not all trauma-based behaviours are met with appropriate care and intervention, and therefore, these behaviours do not always result in successfully ending the violence. That does not mean that they are not acts of resistance. Trauma-based behaviours may be the only means available for resisting violence. They are a last resort in drawing attention to ongoing violence which is unnamed and unaddressed. Given a lack of options and support, it is important to recognize the brilliance and necessity of trauma-based behaviours. These behaviours again and again draw attention to that which we are taught to ignore.

My cutting and overdosing, far from being pathological behaviours, were my only source of power. I was a child, dependent upon adults who forced me to live with an overwhelming threat to my safety and bodily autonomy. My attempts to fight and flee, to call for help and to hide, were not successful in protecting me from the danger I was in. Yet my trauma, my body's unwillingness to reflect the distorted reality of my parents, offered up another possibility for escape. Like a dam breaking, my trauma was a force that could not be contained. It was my ultimate refusal of the false narrative of a safe and happy home. It was my refusal to accept what I was experiencing as normal or okay, even as I cognitively began to accept it. My body said no. My trauma created a way out, a loud, unmistakable refusal. Returning to Berne's important assertion that we are powerful not despite the complexities of our bodies, but because of them: I am powerful because of my trauma, not despite it.[9] My trauma is not a failing. My trauma is a way to survive.

Along with resisting violence, the embodied experience of trauma can produce new ways of relating to the world. One of the ways trauma does this is in relation to experiences of time. Trauma queers linear, chronological time, opening up possibilities for time travel.

Many aspects of the embodied experience of trauma are temporal. Flashbacks, nightmares, intrusive thoughts, amnesia, body memories, structural dissociation, hypervigilance, derealization, depersonalization, and ongoing disorientation in time, all demonstrate queer temporalities. The straightforward expectation of time unfolding in a linear progression from the past, to the present, to the future is ruptured by trauma. The past can happen right now. The future can happen right now. In fact, in the traumatized experience of time, the present can be the hardest moment to access.

Flashbacks, nightmares, and intrusive thoughts are experiences of the past as the present; past experiences of violence are experienced as if they are happening in the

---

[9] ibid

present. Amnesia, body memories, and structural dissociation represent a rupture in the seamless narrative of chronological time. Memories may be absent, partial, experienced as sensations without an attached narrative, or may be sectioned off in different parts of the personality. This strangeness can be disorienting, overwhelming, and confusing. It can also release us from the dominant narratives about what time is and how it works, allowing us to relate to time in more creative and intentional ways.

Hypervigilance is an experience of the past as the present as the future. The past is made manifest in the present and the through the past, the future is predicted. In Feminist, Queer, Crip, Alison Kafer writes "'Strange temporalities' could ... include the experiences of those with PTSD ... who live in a kind of anticipatory time, scanning their days for events or exposures that might trigger a response.[10] Such scans include moving both forward and backward in time while remaining present in this moment."[11] Derealization, depersonalization and ongoing experiences of disorientation in time, all have the effect of voiding the 'realness' of time. Rather than a straightforward trajectory with knowable markers along the way, these experiences may seem to happen outside of time, or may not adhere to the objective organization of time. I have shown up at the right place, at the right time, on the wrong day. I have entered a classroom (the right room), looked at the clock (the right time), and felt utterly perplexed by the strangeness of the wrong people sitting in the room with me (the wrong day).

This sort of confusion has a feeling of absurdity to it. It feels strange to be 'out' of time, and unable to get 'in' it. While all of these experiences of the queer temporalities of trauma time are usually framed as negative and dysfunctional, I argue that they represent a different way of being in and relating to the world. They refute the fictitiously objective universal experience of time as linear and chronological, and

---

[10] Kafer, *Feminist, queer, crip.*

[11] ibid

instead open up time as a space that can be moved through in multiple directions. While psychiatric and medical approaches to the 'symptoms' of trauma call for their eventual elimination, I am suggesting an engagement with these embodied experiences which explore their potential.

Kafer points out that disability is often understood temporally in relationship to a potential, future cure.[12] Kafer critiques a "curative imaginary, an understanding of disability that not only expects and assumes intervention but also cannot imagine or comprehend anything other than intervention."[13] My framing of trauma resists this curative imaginary, asking us to stay with the queer temporalities of trauma in order to see what they offer. This time travel of trauma can be painful, but it can also constitute a way of being that is creative, adaptive, and resistant to violence. Time flowing both ways allows for past selves to get what they needed in the past, in the present. It allows for present selves and futures selves to move backward in time, and find new ways of relating to overwhelming experiences with skills and knowledges gained in the future.

As well as queering relationships to time, trauma can create opportunities for intimacies and solidarities with nonhuman beings, including plants, animals, ecosystems, and landscapes. A chapter titled "Following Mercurial Affect" in Mel Chen's Animacies: *Biopolitics, Racial Mattering and Queer Affect* explores how multiple chemical sensitivity, the result of mercury poisoning, has resulted for Chen in an orienting away from the human.[14] Since humans so frequently come with perfume and cigarette smoke, Chen moves toward experiences of intimacy with nonhuman others who do not set off a toxic reaction. Chen writes, "in such a toxic period, anyone or anything that I manage to feel any kind of connection with, whether it's my cat or a chair or a friend or a plant or a stranger or my partner, I think they are, and

---

[12] ibid

[13] ibid

[14] Chen, *Animacies*.

remember they are, all the same ontological thing. What happens to notions of animacy given this lack of distinction between "living" and "lifely" things?"[15]

Trauma can also result in an orientation away from the human. Trauma-based stress responses are set off by stimuli which remind of the original traumas. Because my trauma resulted from violence enacted by humans, it is humans who set off a trauma response in my body. From a young age I developed strong affinities with the nonhuman beings in my environment, including plants, animals, and landscapes. Being outside, away from the adults who abused me, I sought intimacy with those who did me no harm. Trees, bodies of water, birds, animals, and plants of various kinds, constituted the most important relationships in my life.

In particular, much of my abuse happened in a place with a small lake surrounded by forest. Because it was unsafe to sleep in my bed at night I often slept in a tent outside. Awoken by the sunrise I would climb out of my tent and watch the loons landing on the mist covered lake. While I was living an experience of overwhelming terror inside the cottage, I was safe and connected when I was outside with the lake, the trees, and the loons. While I am no longer able to visit this specific place (and that breaks my heart deeply), my relationship to my nonhuman surroundings remain incredibly important to me.

A colonial capitalist worldview objectifies nonhuman beings and does not frame them as potential companions. Trauma can open up the possibility of moving beyond this limited worldview, in order to enter into relationship with a vast number of others. Chen writes "it is only in the recovering of my human-directed sociality that the couch really becomes an unacceptable partner."[16] This... forces me to rethink animacy, since I have encountered an intimacy that does not differentiate, is not dependent on a heartbeat."[17] Discovering an intimacy which "is not dependent on a

---

[15] ibid

[16] ibid

[17] ibid

heartbeat" has utterly transformed my world.[18]

Along with these newfound intimacies, trauma also offers opportunities for more than human solidarities. In a context of impending ecological collapse these solidarities are deeply important. The endless consumption encouraged by capitalism is punctuated with recognitions of that which it is becoming harder and harder to ignore: vast environmental destruction, climate change, and mass extinction. Facing these facts can be incredibly painful and overwhelming.

To relieve this pain, fantasies of untouched, pristine nature are offered at a cost. In "Melancholy Natures, Queer Ecologies", Catriona Sandilands, drawing on the work of Bruce Braun, writes "[an] analysis of the fetishization and commodification of a lost, romanticized nature – 'unspoiled' wilderness – is extremely important... nature becomes a fantasy, a fetish that can be bought to extend the reach of capital rather than prompt criticism of the relationships that produced the loss in the first place."[19] The warning signs of impending ecological collapse are ignored in favour of fantasies which further exacerbate the problem. While capitalism offers the rich fantasies of going "somewhere else," trauma shows us how to stay with what is. There is no other life and no other body than the ones we are living. Likewise there is no other world.

Sandilands asks "What would it mean to consider seriously the environmental present... as a pile of environmental wreckage, constituted and haunted b ymultiple, personal, and deeply traumatic losses...?"[20] I argue that the embodied experience of trauma can offer a vantage point from which to do this work. The traumatized bodymind is also "constituted and haunted by multiple, personal, and deeply traumatic losses."[21] When we turn toward the possibility of trauma, we face both its staggering loss and its rich potential. We grieve

---

[18] ibid

[19] Sandilands (as Mortimer-Sandilands), & Erikson, *Queer ecologies.* p 342.

[20] ibid

[21] ibid

what is lost and we love what is here. We learn to fight for what is still here, while remaining deeply connected to our loss. We must do this same work with our world which is also undergoing massive traumas. Can we love what is here without resorting to the fantasy of escape? Can we stay with the complexity of what is, feel the massive weight of our losses, and still love the wreckage enough to fight for it with everything we have?

The reframing of trauma that I am putting forth, which values the embodied experience of trauma, while resisting the violence that produces it, offers a way to value the world that is here, while resisting the violence that is killing it. Instead of pining after lost pasts and utopian futures, or extending colonial violence in search of enclaves of 'untouched' nature, trauma can offer a way to be with what is here now. In a poem titled "Dirty River Girl," Leah Lakshmi Piepzna-Samarasinha writes about a polluted river in the town where she grew up. She describes how the river was polluted by the factories, and how the toxicity of the river resulted in disablement and death for members of her community.[22] She also describes how trauma from sexual violence can result in disablement, writing, "[there's] an underground river that whispers: / abuse survivors are the ones who get the weird diseases. / the ones who were raped and touched too young, / us whose bodies tell terrible stories, horrible lies."[23]

Yet Piepzna-Samarasinha does not write from a perspective of what Kafer calls the "curative imaginary," orienting toward hope for a cure. Instead, she wants us to stay with these traumatized, disabled bodies, with this polluted river, and to love them as they are.[24] She writes, "[what] would it take for a river that polluted / to be loved?"[25] She then extends this question to ask if "working-class, fucked

[22] Piepzna-Samarasinha, "Dirty river girl."

[23] Piepzna-Samarasinha, "Dirty river girl," p. 30.

[24] Kafer, Feminist, queer, crip.

[25] Piepzna-Samarasinha, "Dirty River Girl", p. 33.

up, sick, survivor bodies" are beautiful just as they are?[26] She asks what it would take "for that river to be loved" and for those bodies "to come back from being swept away."[27] This profound and complex position allows for an engagement with what is. It allows us to love and value what is here, while simultaneously naming and resisting violence.

Trauma can reorient us toward the more than human, ecological world and encourage us to build relationships of intimacy and solidarity. This reorientation toward a living world populated by more than human actors lends itself to the practice of magic. Magic is a worldview in which the universe is alive, active, collaborative, and relational. Magic invites us to reject the deadening of capitalism and to remember that we are in a living world of relationship. Richard Kieckhefer in his book *Magic in the Middle Ages* describes what he terms a "[common] tradition of medieval magic" writing "much of the magic in medieval Europe was distributed widely, and... was not regularly limited to any specific group."[28] This common practice of magic flowed from and upheld a particular worldview in which the cosmos was understood as dynamic, lively, relational, and responsive. Silvia Federici in her book *Caliban and the Witch: Women, the Body and Primitive Accumulation* explores the practice of magic in the Middle Ages, writing,

> At the basis of magic was an animistic conception of nature that did not admit to any separation between matter and spirit, and thus imagined the cosmos as a *living organism*, populated by occult forces, where every element was in "sympathetic" relation with the rest.[29]

---

[26] ibid

[27] ibid

[28] Kieckhefer, *Magic in the Middle Ages*, p. 56-57.

[29] Federici, *Caliban and the Witch*, p. 141-142.

Contemporary practitioners of magic revive this understanding of a living universe. Rejecting worldviews which objectify the world and strip it of its mystery and power, contemporary practitioners of magic honour and respond to a world of mystery that is very much alive. Sabrina Scott in their book *witchbody* considers the practice of magic in a contemporary context, writing, "[magical] practitioners notice the work of nonhumans and ask these nonhuman bodies to work with them in magic, in the co-creation of existence."[30] Magic continues today to be a collaborative practice situated in a living universe. This magic can be grounded in the embodied experience of trauma. A bodymind which defies linear logics and embraces strange intimacies is a bodymind rich with magical potential.

Trauma magic is magic rooted in the particular embodied experiences of trauma. It is magic that draws on the difference trauma offers and employs it toward magical ends. Trauma magic refutes reductive and objectifying representations of the world, replacing them with acknowledgment of the power of more than human actors. Trauma magic grows out of experiences of pain and is committed to liberation. It is my experience of trauma which leads me to magic. It is my queer relationship to time and my orientation toward more than human collaborators, among other aspects of my embodied experience of trauma, which result in my particular practice of magic. It is my experiences of violence that commit me to a magical practice invested in justice for all who are traumatized, human and nonhuman alike. Trauma magic is just one example of the possibilities which open up when we decide to stay with trauma and value what it offers us.

The concept 'trauma' can be mobilized in harmful ways by validating some violences while naturalizing others, and by creating a focus on individual healing rather than justice at a systemic level. Despite these harmful deployments of trauma, it is necessary to have a word with which to describe the embodied, ongoing experience of disablement which can

---

[30] Scott, *witchbody*, p. 10.

be experienced by survivors of violence. Remaining critical of harmful deployments of trauma, I seek an analysis of trauma which foregrounds liberation. An important part of this is valuing embodied experiences of trauma while simultaneously calling attention to and resisting ongoing violence. Theories within critical disability studies have suggested that disability can be understood as desirable[31], as an offering[32], and as something to move toward.[33] Rather than framing disabled embodiment as tragic, unwanted, or less than nondisabled embodiment, disability theorists have reframed disability as valuable in its own right, and rich with its own possibilities.

This reframing is an important project which seeks to undo ableist scripts and to create space in which to imagine disability as wanted, welcomed, and loved. Yet trauma has largely been left out of these imaginings. This, I argue, is because trauma is associated with its origins, usually violence. How can disability produced through violence be framed as desirable? Would valuing and loving the embodied result of violence mean condoning the violence itself? In "Meditations on Natural Worlds, Disabled Bodies and a Politics of Cure," Eli Clare writes, "when the woman whose body has been shaped by military pollution declares, 'I hate the military and love my body,' she is saying something brand new and deeply complex."[34] It is this complexity that I am seeking. The embodied experience of trauma, rather than being framed as an undesirable and unfortunate result of violence, can be reframed as a creative way of being in the world, rich with potential.

It is possible and necessary to name and resist violence, while valuing the disabled embodiment of trauma. Our lives, minds, and bodies are the only ones we have, and we deserve to value and love them. The violence we have experienced has changed us, but we are not that violence. In fact, our

---

[31] McRuer, *Crip theory*.

[32] Ndopu, "Don't deny me my disability, dignity, and equal opportunity."

[33] Mingus, "Moving toward the ugly."

[34] Clare, "Meditations on natural worlds, disabled bodies and a politics of cure," p. 15

changing in response to violence has been a brilliant strategy of resistance to violence. Trauma resists the violence that produces it. It also opens up possibilities for different ways of being in the world.

Trauma can queer time by refusing to comply with linear, chronological renditions of time, imagining time instead as a space that can be moved through in any direction. Trauma offers possibilities for more than human intimacies and solidarities, by orienting away from the human, and by creating space for the complexity of loving what is here while working for change. Trauma can lend itself to a particular form of magic, a spiritual, collaborative practice that honours and collaborates with a living universe. When we stay with trauma long enough to consider its possibilities we begin the work of valuing the difference trauma brings. We can meet our disabled, traumatized bodies, and our injured, traumatized world, where they are. This honesty, this willingness to value, love, and work with what is, resists the "curative imaginary."[35]

Instead of seeking out pristine, untouched nature, or dreaming of what might have been if we had not experienced the violence we did, we can really be with what is here. Queer time, trauma magic, and more than human solidarities are some of the generative and wondrous aspects of what is here. It is from this place that we can resist violence, and create new ways of being in the world.

---

[35] Kafer, *Feminist, queer, crip*, p. 27.

Fairies in Ontario:

Locality, Diaspora, and Ecological Ethics

In grade six, I was a weird kid, strange and lonely, full of pain and hope. I was surviving abuse to the best of my ability, and I was in love with the mystery and magic of the world. One of my favourite novels was *The Moorchild* by Eloise McGraw.[36] It told the story of a changeling, a fairy child left in place of a human child taken by the fairies. Named Molq by the fairies and renamed Saaski by the humans, the changeling child felt profoundly out of place. Rejected by the fairies for being unable to perform particular fairy tasks, she was not quite human either. As a strange and troubled child who likewise did not quite fit anywhere, this book spoke to me deeply. I identified with the changeling and drew strength from a protagonist who occupied such a liminal space.

This liminality drew me toward fairies. They were powerful, magical, and they moved between worlds. I imagined them playing in the fields and forests which surrounded my home, existing in this reality one moment, the next vanishing from sight. My younger cousin reports that I solemnly declared that fairies did indeed inhabit the forest we spent our time playing in. She believed me at my word. My younger sister developed an interest in trying to lure leprechauns out of hiding in our backyard by leaving them attractive gifts. The space at the end of our driveway and the time spent waiting for the school bus to appear over the hill down the road combined in a particularly potent spacial-temporal liminality in which we had a number of supernatural experiences. We witnessed a grackle cast the shadow of a horse. We watched the sky fill with striking shapes of a starling murmuration. And once, I saw a fairy.

I saw the fairy for only a moment but I told the story of this encounter many times. Just across the road from where I stood waiting for the school bus to arrive, among the strewn autumn leaves, I witnessed a small creature, about three inches tall, dancing wildly. The creature was mud-green all over, wearing no discernable clothing, with no discernable features. In fact, strangely, the creature appeared to be

---

[36] McGraw, *The Moorchild*.

two-dimensional, a flat cut-out moving in a three-dimensional world. Over the years I told and retold the story of my encounter with conviction to believing children who shared stories of their own fairy encounters. As I grew older my listeners became more and more skeptical.

Eventually, I became skeptical of myself. Perhaps I had made it up after all. Perhaps it was just a story I had told so many times I had convinced myself it was true. I became an adult and left the fairies behind, believing them to be the fruits of an overactive childhood imagination. I was not aware that my Irish ancestors had relationships with fairies all throughout their adult lives. I did not know that my beloved favourite novel *The Moorchild* was based on folklore that structured my Irish ancestors' worldview. Like many in the Irish diaspora my roots to the land of my ancestors had long ago been severed. Even in Ireland, fairy beliefs no longer hold the power that they once did, although they have not disappeared.

In my teenage years getting drunk became more important than finding fairies. A winding road took me through many years of addiction and despair. Wrestling with childhood trauma, complex ptsd, and alcoholism, I eventually turned to spirituality in order to survive. I came to embrace magic in my adult life. I found magic in strange places: the discarded image of the Virgin Mary found in the trash, the Twelve Steps which led me out of the nightmare of addiction, the lit candles on my altar, the whispered words of prayer, synchronicity full with meaning, the moon which hung in the sky hallowed by rainbow light, my very breath which moved through my body still. I found magic in the way I moved through the liminal space of time, ducking in and out of this time line, moving forward and backward. I found magic in my trauma, in my will to live creatively and tenaciously, despite the many obstacles I had to overcome. I came to understand myself as a witch. Spirituality returned as a central, life sustaining part of me. It came back the way breath does.

I discovered that skepticism could not sustain me but magic could. My interest in the spiritual worldviews of my ancestors took on importance. I started to think about the magic that animated my childhood with more than skepticism and derision. I began to reconsider fairies. That small, dancing, two-dimensional creature had shown me something, offered me something. And I was ready to return to that lesson.

I learned that in Ireland people have had reciprocal relationships with fairies for hundreds of years. Even today fairy bushes are left undisturbed in the middle of farmed fields. Diarmuid Ó Giolláin explains,

> The respect given to 'lone bushes' or 'fairy bushes' has long been attested to; they still often stand unmolested in the middle of a cultivated field. The fairy bush was usually a rowan, holly, elderberry or whitethorn which stood alone in a field rather than in a hedgetow, and thus apparently was not planted by human hand..."[37]

Far from being a silly, childhood fantasy, fairies were an integral part of the belief system of my ancestors. Remnants of this belief system survive in Ireland today. When I was visiting County Mayo, Ireland, while having dinner with the family of a friend, someone asked if we could see the fairy fort that was located on the property. The response was, "Oh no, we never go out there after six. In the evenings the fairies are out doing their things and we leave them alone." It is difficult to know how seriously to take this statement, but we did not go out to the fort.

Talk of fairies in Canada is easily dismissed as childish or ridiculous, but fairies provoke very different feelings in Ireland. Fairies are creatures who demand respect. This relationship of respect shapes the Irish landscape and the worldview of the Irish people. While talk of fairies in Ireland today may be done somewhat tongue in cheek, fairies are not beings to laugh at. Despite literal belief in fairies being in

[37] Ó Giolláin, "The fairy belief and official religion in Ireland," p.199.

decline, the traditional respect for fairies continues to shape the Irish people and the Irish landscape, as indicated by the farmer leaving the fairybush undisturbed and the unwillingness of my friend's family to go near the fairy fort after 6pm.

Fairy belief is an ancient part of "Irish popular religion," which predates Christianity in Ireland.[38] Rather than disappearing with the introduction of Christianity in the early Middle Ages, fairy belief adapted to and intermingled with the new Christian belief system.[39] The two belief systems continue to exist side by side to this day. The fairy faith grows out of an oral tradition of storytelling,[40] and is deeply tied to the land.[41] Ó Giolláin describes the importance of "sacred sites in the countryside… Most numerous [of which] are the thirty or forty thousand forts or raths, mostly in fact Iron Age ring forts, commonly called 'fairy forts,' whose strong otherworld associations have helped to preserve them to the present day."[42] The fairy forts and raths, like the fairybushes, are part of an enchanted landscape. This landscape includes "caverns, hills, islands, rocks, trees, water bodies and wells" which are believed to be inhabited by fairies.[43] Fairy beliefs are not abstract; they exist as part of the material world. For the Irish people, relationships with land have shaped stories and beliefs about fairies. Likewise, relationships with fairies have shaped relationships with the land.

Patrivia Lysaght in her study of the storytelling of Mrs. Jenny McGlynn, of Mountmellick, County Laoise, Ireland, highlights the importance of the physical landscape to the fairy faith.[44] She writes,

---

[38] ibid

[39] ibid

[40] Ballard, "Fairies and the supernatural on Reachrai" and Lysaght, "Fairylore from the Midlands of Ireland."

[41] LaViolette, & Mcintosh, "Fairy hills: merging heritage and conservation," and Ó Giolláin, "The fairy belief and official religion in Ireland."

[42] Ó Giolláin, "The fairy belief and official religion in Ireland," p. 199.

[43] LaViolette, & Mcintosh, "Fairy hills: merging heritage and conservation."

[44] Lysaght, "Fairylore from the Midlands of Ireland."

> Jenny's professed belief in the existence of the fairy world ... is centred around the existence in her immediate neighborhood of a rath or mound, traditionally considered a dwelling place of the fairy race. It is probably fair to say that this particular landscape feature is a *sine qua non* for Jenny's fairy beliefs.[45]

Fairy beliefs are embedded in the land itself. Physical spaces like the rath in McGlynn's neighborhood mark the presence of fairies. As a land based spirituality, the fairy faith elicits particular relationships to the land. Spaces known to belong to the fairies are treated with respect, reverence, or fear. Lysaght explains, "To Jenny these are sacred places and should be treated with respect."[46] LaViolette and McIntosh discuss the various spaces associated with fairies writing

> Certain taboos were often associated with these places relating to the belief that fairies inhabited them. Most typically these were concerned with restricting their access, especially at threshold times such as dawn and dusk, as well as restricting the removal of earth, stones, and timber.[47]

The fairy faith, embedded in the landscape, requires that humans behave with respect. A fairybush will not be cut down even it stands in a farmer's field, and a fort must not be disturbed.

To the Irish, "[the] fairies were a part of life."[48] Interactions with the fairies were, and in some cases still are, a commonplace part of existence. The fairy faith requires a reciprocal, respectful relationship with the fairies. Ó Giolláin

---

[45] ibid, p. 30.

[46] Lysaght, "Fairylore from the Midlands of Ireland."

[47] LaViolette, & Mcintosh, "Fairy hills: merging heritage and conservation," p. 4.

[48] Ó Giolláin, "The fairy belief and official religion in Ireland," p. 20.

(1991) explains that "they called to the door to borrow meal, they enlisted the help of mortal midwives, they lent their cows, they saved people from death and bestowed magical gifts."[49] The fairies could offer help or be in need of human help. They could also cause harm. Fairies might prevent a cow from giving milk, a serious consequence in a culture heavily dependent on dairy.[50] Fairies might make humans fall ill.[51] They might even take a human child and leave a changeling in its place.[52] Fairies are capable of a great deal of harm, ranging from simple mischief, to the taking of a life. These punishments could result from any form of disrespect toward the fairies, including "an incursion onto a rath... disturbing a fairy tree, building a house in the wrong place" and other such infractions.[53]

Respect toward the fairies is demonstrated in a number of ways. Ó Giolláin writes "Due respect was shown to them by speaking of them in a flattering way (the 'good people,' 'the gentry')...."[54] Other ways of demonstrating respect include "warning them before throwing out the dirty water at night... making sure not to build over their houses or paths... not mocking them... [and] making offerings to them."[55] Linda-May Ballard also describes a "commonly held belief that the fairies should not be sought out or interfered with, that it is dangerous to enquire into their nature and by implication, into their elemental and fundamental significance."[56] Demonstrating respect toward the fairies, in action, word

---

[49] ibid

[50] Jenkins, "Witches and fairies: Supernatural aggression and deviance among the Irish peasantry."

[51] ibid

[52] Lysaght, "Fairylore from the Midlands of Ireland," Ó Giolláin, "The fairy belief and official religion in Ireland," and Jenkins, "Witches and fairies: Supernatural aggression and deviance among the Irish peasantry."

[53] Jenkins, "Witches and fairies: Supernatural aggression and deviance among the Irish peasantry." p. 316.

[54] Ó Giolláin, "The fairy belief and official religion in Ireland," p. 201.

[55] Ó Giolláin, "The fairy belief and official religion in Ireland," p. 202.

[56] Ballard, "Fairies and the supernatural on Reachrai" p. 56.

and adherence to taboo, is an important aspect of the reciprocal relationship between fairies and humans.

Discovering that my childhood belief in fairies held echoes of my ancestors' worldview led me to reconsider belief in fairies. I saw that my willingness to dismiss fairies disconnected me from the spiritual knowledge of my ancestors. It was also disrespectful to the fairies, something which I now realized was serious and dangerous business. In reconsidering fairy beliefs, I came to understand the importance of the fairy faith within Irish history, culture, religion, and relationship to the land. I realized that the oral tradition of telling stories about fairies help to build and strengthen relationships among humans. I saw that the taboo of disturbing the many plants and places in the physical landscape which are inhabited by fairies led to an ecological ethics in which the land must be treated with respect. The fairy faith is a worldview of relationship: relationships between humans, fairies, and the land.

As a person of Irish descent whose family has lived in Canada for generations I am deeply disconnected from the spiritual knowledge of my ancestors. I believe that relearning these knowledges is important. Yet how do I reconnect with a place-based spirituality when I am no longer in that place? I am not in Ireland, among the raths and the fairybushes. The landscapes and plants which surround me are different from those which surrounded my ancestors.

I have lived my whole life in a landscape of seasons: winters bright white with snow, summers hot enough to make the air squiggle with humidity, the long muddy springs, and the autumns with trees ablaze. This is the land that I know and love, the land I am in deep relationship with, the land that has loved me back and sustained me since I was born. I had the opportunity to visit Ireland once. It is stunning and the land is alive with the stories of my ancestors, but Ireland is not my home.

I grew up and have spent most of my life in Southern Ontario, land that also holds the stories of my ancestors, and that holds the older and ongoing stories of the Anishinabek, the Haudenosaunee, and the Wendat peoples. Being a settler growing up in a colonial country, I was not told the stories of the place where I lived. It wasn't until I was adult that I learned about the One Spoon, One Dish wampum, a treaty between the Anishinabek and Haudenosaunee Confederacies. This treaty is an agreement to 'eat with one spoon', meaning that everyone should share the resources, and not take more than the land can sustain. I now live in Montréal, or Tio'Tia:ke, which represents the Eastern Door of the Haudenosaunee Confederacy.

Settler colonial countries like Canada maintain their claims to legitimacy in part by hiding history: by keeping the stories, the treaties, and the truth from the people who live here. The Indigenous peoples of Turtle Island are engaged in massive cultural and language revival projects, bringing back to life what the genocidal colonial nation states tried to obliterate. For settlers whose families have lived here for many generations, we often lack knowledge both about the history of the places where we live today and the history of the places where we come from. Capitalism and settler colonialism encourage a dissociated relationship to land and place. Land based cultures and spiritual knowledges offer ways to enter into reciprocal relationship with land.

Like many settlers, once I came into consciousness about the genocidal nation state in which I live, I began to question the legitimacy of my own relationship to this land. Could I really claim a loving reciprocal relationship to this place? Could I even really call this place my home? What is my responsibility to the land, and to the First Nations that Canada tried to drive out of existence in order to secure its colonial rule? Is it possible to use the forgotten knowledges of my ancestors from the far away land of Ireland to animate an ethical relationship with this place, here? Rather than collapse into shame, I step forward with a sense of love, belonging, and responsibility. The knowledges of my ancestors help me to be a responsible member of the communities I move through here and now.

Environmental destruction is enabled in part by a

deep alienation from the land. Finding ways to overcome that alienation and to enter into respectful, ethical relationship with the land is important ecological work. As capitalism treats the planet as a resource, threatening the future viability of human life here, this work has never been more important. For many, spiritual traditions play an important role in that work. Robin Wall Kimmerer writes,

> In a colonist society the ceremonies that endure are not about the land; they are about family and culture, values that are transportable from the old country. Ceremonies for the land no doubt existed there, but it seems they did not survive emigration in any substantial way. I think there is wisdom in regenerating them here, as a means to form bonds with this land.[57]

Reviving the fairy faith in Canada offers a possibility for engaging with this land in ethical, respectful ways, ways which are rooted in my own ancestry and culture. There are good reasons for reviving the fairy faith in Canada, but are there even fairies here?

Recognizing that fairies were known to live in very particular places in the Irish landscape led me to believe that I was not likely to find fairies in Canada, despite my childhood experiences. I am far away from the raths and fairy bushes my ancestors lived among. Recently, in one of my classes, we were discussing mushrooms. I talked about fairy rings, circular patterns of mushrooms which are known in Ireland to be entrances into the Other World. Someone asked if fairy rings were found in Canada. I didn't know. My professor informed me that she had seen a fairy ring in Ontario. She then looked it up online and confirmed that there are indeed species of mushrooms in Ontario which grew in circular rings. This struck a chord with me. Perhaps there were fairies in Canada after all.

---

[57] Kimmerer, *Braiding sweetgrass*, p. 250.

Peter Narváez quotes Richard M. Dorson as writing that fairies "cavorted and made mischief throughout the isles of Britain, but failed to take passage with the emigrants sailing for America."[58] According to Dorson fairies were "too closely associated with the culture and the geography of the Old Country to migrate."[59] Narváez explains that "While fairylore has been extensively studied by European folklorists, it is generally assumed that fairies have not existed in North America."[60] This fits with my initial thought that creatures so situated in a particular landscape, and a belief system so rooted in relationship to that landscape, might not be able to exist elsewhere. Yet Narváez goes on to describe a "large amount of fairylore apparent in Newfoundland."[61] Irish settler communities in Newfoundland continued to have relationships with fairies even as they no longer lived in Ireland.

Gary R. Butler writes about a surviving fairy tradition in French-Newfoundland. This tradition has all but disappeared, yet he found people who remember the *lutin*.[62] Discussing the fairy belief of the Simons, a couple he interviewed, both of whom were in their seventies at the time, Butler writes "the Simons accept what they had been told by past generations concerning the lutins.... Nevertheless, they do not regard the lutin as a reality in their present environment, but see it as a phenomenon which ceased to exist at some point in the past."[63] According to the Simons, there were once fairies in Newfoundland, but they seem to no longer be there. Narváez likewise describes fairy belief disappearing in Irish Newfoundland communities writing "Until relatively recently, fairies in Newfoundland have been realities because news of them circulated in vigorous oral tradition and

---

[58] Narváez, "Newfoundland berry pickers 'in the fairies,'" p. 339.

[59] Dorson in Narváez, "Newfoundland berry pickers 'in the fairies,'" p. 339.60

[60] Narváez, "Newfoundland berry pickers 'in the fairies,'" p. 339.

[61] ibid

[62] Butler, G. R. "The lutin tradition in French-Newfoundland culture: Discourse and belief."

[63] ibid, p. 12.

firsthand evidence of their activity was readily available."[64] Now, however, we have "dismissed fairies from our view."[65] So fairies have existed on the east coast of Canada and people have had relationships with them there. In both French and Irish communities fairies have played an active role on this side of the ocean.

Yet the fairies seem to be disappearing. Fairy belief is fading, not only in Newfoundland, but in Ireland as well.[66] Ó Giolláin writes,

> Though legends of the fairies can still be heard in Ireland today, few of them are set in very recent times. People do not experience the fairies much anymore.... Rural communities now have little or no cultural or economic autonomy... and are to an extent merely passive receivers of an international or hegemonic 'mass culture'.... An exaltation of localism, the fairy belief cannot survive in such a climate.[67]

Alienation from land, community, and culture result in the disappearance of fairies. A remembrance of fairies might result in a remembrance of land, community, and culture, opening people to ethical relationship with place. Remembering fairies in Canada might allow settlers whose ancestors practiced the fairy faith to enter into ethical relationship with this land.

While I had discovered that people had entered into relationships with fairies on the east coast of Canada, I wondered if fairies were found in Ontario, the land that I grew up on. My childhood experience would indicate that fairies are found there, but I was curious to know if the fairy faith had, at one point, taken root in Ontario. Was I the only one with a story of a fairy encounter in Ontario? I did some

---

[64] Narváez, "Newfoundland berry pickers 'in the fairies,'" p. 360.

[65] ibid

[66] Ó Giolláin, "The fairy belief and official religion in Ireland."

[67] Ó Giolláin, "The fairy belief and official religion in Ireland," p. 211.

research and came across an article in *The Journal of American Folklore* written in 1918 by Katherine H. Wintemberg and W. J. Wintemberg, titled "Folk-Lore from Grey County, Ontario."[68] Wintemberg and Wintermberg write "The following collection of folk-lore material was made in a Scotch-Irish community in Normanby township, Grey County, Ontario, where the Irish element preponderates."[69] A list of local stories about fairies is given, including,

> A fairy once came to a house asking for a dish of meal. The women gave her some. The dish was returned, and ever after it was never empty.... Those who had the temerity to dig in a fairy mound or fort had their heads turned around, and they were kept in this position until they desisted.... a man who did not believe in fairies, and who insisted on using a piece of ground fenced off and set aside for their use... stuck his spade into the ground and found he could not pull it out again.[70]

These, and other stories, indicate a thriving fairy faith in an Irish-Scottish community in Ontario in 1918. Like the stories of fairies told in Ireland, these stories pass on important information about right relationship with the fairies and with the land. Fairies exist in Ontario but memory of them is fading, as it is in Ireland. Through the process of assimilation, much Irish culture and religion was lost in the Irish diaspora, prompting a more thorough loss of fairy faith in the diaspora than in Ireland.

My childhood belief in fairies was a response to the fragments of the fairy faith which found their way to me. My openness to fairies led me to a fairy encounter. This encounter was an invitation to remembrance and relationship. The

---

[68] Wintemberg & Wintemberg, "Folk-lore from Grey County, Ontario."

[69] ibid, p. 83.

[70] ibid, p. 104.

disenchantment of adulthood led me astray, but I have found my way back to the fairies. Reviving the fairy faith is not an easy task. It requires openness to an enchanted worldview which is not taken seriously today. It also requires the telling of stories. The fairy faith grows out of a rich oral tradition and an intimate relationship with the land. Modern day colonialism and capitalism alienate us from each other and from the land.

Relationship, the fundamental reality of the fairy faith, is difficult to sustain in a culture of alienation. Yet the reasons why it would be difficult to revive the fairy faith are also reasons why doing so is important. Remembering the fairies is a means of reviving relationship, with the land, with community, and with fairies themselves. Fairies remind us to behave with respect. They remind us that the trees, hills, fields, and forests are not our property. They remind us to practice humility and to leave fairybushes untouched, even if they appear in a farmer's field. They provoke us to remember a sense of awe and reverence at the mystery of the living world around us. They encourage us to tell stories and build community by sharing knowledge. They invite us into ethical, ecological and communal relationships, with ourselves, with each other, with the spaces we move through, and with the beings who share those spaces, including the Good People themselves.

Can Theory
Be a Spell?
(Part One)

Can theory be a spell?

To form words with letters. *Teach children to spell.*
Intransitive verb.
To add up to. *Crop failure spells famine.* Transitive verb.
To find out by study or come to understand. *Spell out directions.* Transitive verb.
A state of enchantment. *To be put under a spell.* Noun.

Spells have power. They take letters and make words which have meaning. What is that other than magic? When the crop failure spells famine that is a powerful force. The dictionary seems to have forgotten the noun usage of spell as a period of time. Wait for a spell. What is the significance of a spell of time? To spell out is to explain, to create understanding. Spelling means to make meaning, whether we are spelling a word or spelling out directions. To cast a spell is to enact "a strong compelling influence or attraction."[71] Spells are enchantment. Spells are power. Spells are the ability to influence, to change. Spells make things happen.

Can theory be a spell?

I leave my magic in the backyard where the squirrels chase each other in circles, where, under full moons I set up my candles and sit on the earth, where the garden struggles against slugs and squirrels, where I try to strengthen my green thumb, my plant magic. I leave my magic in the kitchen with my jars upon jars of herbs, with my oil and oregon grape root infusion sitting on the window sill soaking up sun, with my apple cider vinegar tinctures, with the blessings, expressions of gratitude, and intentions I make when I eat. I leave my magic in my 12 step meetings, where people say "it was a god moment", "I can feel my higher power working in my life", "when I let go, I can feel things start to happen", where we talk about prayer, how our spiritual practice is today, where we listen with full and open hearts and enact the magic of

---

[71] Merriam-Webster, 2015.

saving our lives, where we hold hands and pray. I leave my magic in conversations with other witches, where it enlivens the way we discuss everyday things, where, in fact, there is no distinction between magic and everyday things, where we talk about our practices, our craft, where we talk about the messages we are picking up, the lesson we are learning. I leave my magic at my altar where I sit each morning and write, where I sit each morning and ask for help, where I sit each night and say thank you, where I light my candles, lay down my tarot cards, listen to what comes to me. I leave my magic pressed between the pages of books, alive on city streets and in alleyways, in the lake, the river, the sky, in my pulse, my fingertips, my sexuality, in the synchronicity and connectedness I feel all around me and inside me, when I open myself to it.

I leave my magic. I do not bring it into the university.

I ask my friend Sabrina if they bring their magic into the university. They do. They have found a way to bring magic there, to engage with magic there, to be present with magic there. They admit that it is difficult, but they encourage me to try. I am afraid. I am forgetful. I mention being a witch and then I don't know how to follow through. I don't know how to bring my magic to my theory, how to bring my theory to my magic. Sabrina suggests showing up to the classroom early, walking around it, paying attention to energies. They say "bring candles if you need to." But I am afraid. I don't know why I am so afraid.

Can theory be a spell?

I know poetry can be.
In my poetry my magic is alive and flourishing.
I sidestep the question of magic
and decide to bring my poetry into my theory,
to invite my creative practice into conversation
with my academic one.

I choose two professors to work with
over the summer who are both creative and
encouraging, who invite me to explore scholarship in
unusual ways.
I read "Lyric Inquiry" by Lorri Neilsen.
I feel a stirring deep inside of me.
I try to write.
I can't write.
I freeze.
I procrastinate for days,
then weeks.
I am stuck.

I meet with one of the professors I am working with.
We discuss the film project I am working on,
how I feel out of my depth.
We discuss the project of bringing my creative work
and my academic work into conversation with each
other.
I tell her I am stuck. I don't know what the outcome
will be.
She tells me to think like a plant.
Follow the light.
Follow the water.

All Generations Will Call Me Blessed:

A Queer Marian Devotion

I found her likeness in the garbage: a ceramic sculpture of the Holy Virgin, in the trash. Taken by her, I took her likeness home. She hangs above my altar to this day.

A queer witch who practices Marian devotion may seem a contradiction. Yet Our Lady of Mercy has always welcomed me with her whole heart. I was not raised Catholic, but my ancestors are Irish Catholic stretching back generations. When I practice Marian devotion, I am aligning my practice with theirs. I find great comfort and power in my practice of Marian devotion yet, as Sian Taylder explains,

> Marian devotion... has long been the domain of a traditional and conservative Catholicism that has suppressed women and denied them their sexuality. Mary's role in this conspiracy has been self-evident, offering women an impossible and contradictory model which makes them agents of their own oppression.[72]

As a virgin and a mother, Mary can be misused to demand impossible, contradictory standards of femininity. She can be misused by those who dishonour her to shame and repress feminine sexuality. Despite this, I do not feel shamed or repressed by Mary. I was not raised Catholic like my ancestors were, and I have a different relationship to her from those who did not have a choice in their Christianity. I know that for many the relationship with Mary can be convoluted through the patriarchal messages of the Catholic church, but I know also that people come to her with things they would never bring to God. I am invested in freeing Mary from the patriarchal grasp of the church and releasing her queer and feminist potential. This paper seeks out that potential by employing what Sally Cunneen calls "an imaginative feminist lens", reading between the lines of Marian devotion to find her queerness, her pleasure, and her power.[73]

Revisioning Our Lady of Mercy requires a willingness

---

[72] Taylder, "Our lady of the libido: Towards a Marian Theology of sexual liberation?" p. 345.

[73] Cunneen, "Breaking Mary's silence: A feminist reflection on Marian piety." p. 321.

to engage with her creatively. It requires a willingness to look beyond the official narratives of the Catholic church, to the lived practice of Marian devotion. In order to access Mary's queer, feminist potential we must be willing to listen to her in her many forms, as Our Lady of Sorrows, as the Queen of Heaven, and as the Holy Virgin, Mother of God. We must be willing to think metaphorically and imaginatively, and to hold contradiction with grace. Cunneen reminds us that "women have probably always related in ways other than those officially suggested to them, and that their views are slowly being incorporated into mainstream understanding of her significance."[74] The intimate, day to day experience of prayer and devotion diverges from the officially sanctioned narratives of the Church. In this personal, emotional space, new meanings are made for Mary, meanings unsanctioned and in some cases scandalous. All the same, these meanings are the lived meanings of those in devotion to her, and they have a life of their own.

Maaike de Haardt writes that "theological reflection should not only be concerned with theological utterances, judgements and discussions, but just as much with research on the theological relevance of 'religious practices' and 'lived faith.'"[75] How people live their faith in the day to day is so much more alive and present than the instructions they are given by authorities about how they should live their faith. The personal relationships people develop with Mary can stray quite far from the sanctioned place of Mary within the Church. This lived faith can reveal aspects of Mary which are not included in official Church doctrine. According to de Haardt, taking lived faith seriously allows "Other dimensions and images to emerge, wherein mostly unnamed dimensions of the divine can be brought up for discussion."[76] Resisting the Church's monopoly on Mariology can take the form of taking Marian devotion seriously. In practice we find a rich array of meaning attached to the Holy Virgin. As a queer,

---

[74] ibid

[75] de Haardt, "The Marian paradox: Marian practices as a road to a new Mariology?" p. 174.

[76] ibid

feminist witch, the meaning I discover here resonates with me deeply.

Mary is both sacred and human; she is both heavenly and historical. For many, her humanity makes her approachable and relatable. She is not a perfect or disembodied God. Like us, she was made of flesh and blood. She lived and died. Her humanity offers a way to relate to the divine from the location of being human. She offers an image of divinity in the flesh. Not only was Mary a human being like we are, she was also an oppressed human being. She was poor, young, and pregnant. She walked under the stars, pregnant and seeking a place to give birth. She gave birth to her child in a manger.

Mary is not at the top of any hierarchy. Instead she represents an image of the divine which is of the people. Taylder writes of Mary's frequently invoked titled "'Our Lady' with its implications that Mary belongs to and is part of the community and does not pertain to any particular expression of Catholicism."[77] Our Lady, the Virgin Mary offers us divinity which is human, relatable, and approachable. She offers us a practice of devotion which holds space for the experiences of being human and being oppressed. As Taylder explains

> 'Our' Lady suggests a woman who identifies with and understands what it means to be excluded, oppressed, despised, persecuted. Although we may exalt her as the Queen of Heaven, Star of the Sea she is simultaneously one of us: mother, sister, and friend: companion, *comadre, compañera* and confidante to all those who suffer.[78]

Mary is one of us. She knows the pain of persecution. She knows the trials of being human. Therefore, Mary opens herself to our queer, feminist imaginings as a companion in struggle and a friend in times of suffering. Cunneen quotes Bobbye Burke as writing "[Mary] belonged to the people, not

---

[77] Taylder, "Our lady of the libido: Towards a Marian Theology of sexual liberation?" p. 350-351.

[78] ibid, p. 351.

to the hierarchical church."[79]

While the emphasis is usually placed on Mary's virginity and motherhood, this does not sum up all of who she is. Even from the times of the early Christian Church, there were differences between the image of Mary promoted by men in power, and the Mary which women devoted themselves to. Cunneen explains that the "male fantasy of a quiet, selfless woman may not... have convinced [women] as much as a more available figure of Mary from popular culture."[80] This more widely available figure of Mary was that of Mary as student. Cunneen writes that the "Protevangelium depicted Mary entering the temple to study when she was three, and the theme became a popular and continuing one in art."[81] During the times of the early Christian church, women "could gain an education only as consecrated virgins and widows.... such women were able to lead meaningful lives of scholarship and service, strengthened by their devotion to Mary as a lifelong learner."[82] Historical and contemporary practices of Marian devotion remind us that Mary is complex. While her role as Virgin Mother of God is important, she is multifaceted and offers much to those who seek here. I write these words before a candle lit in a practice of devotion to her, remembering her not only as Divine Mother, but also as student and lifelong learner.

Mary's virginity is also undeniably important. However, it is worth taking the time to reflect on what virginity means. While it is easy to assume that virginity simply means never having had sex, a closer look reveals deeper meanings. Cunneen argues that Mary's virginity signifies her autonomy.[83] She quotes Sojourner Truth as saying "[where] did your Christ come from? ... From God and a woman! Man had nothing to do with him."[84] Mary's virginity can be interpreted

---

[79] Burke in Cunneen, "Breaking Mary's silence: A feminist reflection on Marian piety." p. 330.

[80] ibid, p. 326.

[81] ibid, p. 326.

[82] ibid

[83] ibid

[84] Truth in Cunneen, "Breaking Mary's silence: A feminist reflection on Marian piety." p. 327.

as a form of independence, and this interpretation has historical roots. Cunneen explains that "[in] the Mediterranean world from which Mary and the church arose, virginity symbolized... the independence and self-direction of the goddesses, rather than their abstinence from sex."[85] Mary, the Holy Virgin, can be thought of as an independent and autonomous person and mother. Her virginity can signify her self-direction. Choosing to engage with Mary using an imaginative, feminist lens means reconsidering what Mary's virginity might mean. It means retrieving from the Church the power to define and to define differently. Taylder reminds us that

> It might be pertinent to reconsider exactly what virginity means. Far from pertaining exclusively to sexual abstinence, 'virgin' symbolises potential, fertility, fecundity, quite the opposite of ascetic, sacrificial self-denial. Virgin also refers to independence and autonomy, 'belonging-to-no-man' or 'a recreative submission to the demands of instinct.'[86]

Resignifying Mary's virginity is a creative queer and feminist strategy, lifting meanings from Mary that have been repressed by the Church. When we choose to approach Mary creatively and with openness, we discover that many aspects of her are not what they appear. Marian devotion opens up possibilities for new encounters with Our Lady.

Mary's virginity is often painted as self-sacrificial and denying of sexuality. Likewise Mary is portrayed as humble and self-effacing. She is often represented by the Church as demure, quiet, and passive. Yet this is not the Mary of the New Testament. When Mary goes to Elizabeth to tell her the news of her pregnancy, in a scene referred to as the Magnificat,

---

[85] Cunneen, "Breaking Mary's silence: A feminist reflection on Marian piety."

[86] Taylder, "Our lady of the libido: Towards a Marian Theology of sexual liberation?" p. 350.

she says "My soul magnifies the Lord, / And my spirit has rejoiced in God my Savior. / For He has regarded the lowly state of His maidservant; / For behold, henceforth all generations will call me blessed."[87] While she acknowledges her "lowly state" she also reveres God for his love of the lowly saying "He has put down the mighty from their thrones, / And exalted the lowly. / He has filled the hungry with good things, / And the rich he has sent away empty."[88] As his lowly maidservant she is exalted. She is exalted because God exalts the poor and the hungry. Far from being demure and passive, she possesses strength and power, but her strength and power is in alignment with the poor and the hungry. Cunneen reminds us that the lowliness Mary describes is what makes her 'one of the people', writing "what Mary calls her lowliness is a matter of class and lack of power, placing her (and her son) among those whom God protects."[89] The Magnificat reveals a woman who is powerful, active, and passionate about justice. She speaks of power for the people.

She also states that her soul magnifies the Lord and that all generations will call her blessed. When I first read these words I was surprised. They did not reflect the passive, self-effacing image of Mary I had been taught to see. Instead, these words portray an active, passionate woman who acknowledges her own power. It sounds like Mary is proud, even like she is bragging. She loves to be chosen by God, to be blessed by Him, and to assist Him in His work of casting the mighty from their thrones and lifting up the poor. Cunneen writes "Mary's response to Elizabeth's greeting in her Magnificat is hardly proof of the self-abasement that contemporary women complain about in her. She tells us God has done great things for her and all generations will call her blessed."[90] Her pleasure in this statement is visceral. For a pregnant, unmarried, poor woman to make such a declarative

---

[87] Luke 1:46-55, New King James Version.

[88] Luke 1:46-55, New King James Version.

[89] Cunneen, "Breaking Mary's silence: A feminist reflection on Marian piety." p. 323.

[90] ibid

statement about her power and worth is striking. She will not be forgotten. We will remember her. We will call her blessed.

Along with remembering Mary's power, a queer, feminist analysis of Mary requires that we consider what Mary *does* for those who are devoted to her. Drawing on de Haardt's concept of 'lived faith' we must consider what role Mary plays in the lives of those who remember her and what needs she fulfills.[91] de Haardt writes,

> [anyone], in any condition, may come to [Mary]. The fact that people do indeed turn to Mary with all kinds of physical and mental needs, reveals... a dimension of spirituality and of human life which Western people often prefer to forget: their innate vulnerability and mortality.[92]

de Haardt points out two important things here. Mary holds space for our deepest fears and needs; she honours our human vulnerability. She also turns no one away. Often referred to as Our Lady of Mercy, Mary is kind and welcoming. Unlike the Christian God who is sometimes portrayed as harsh and unapproachable, Mary welcomes all. She is forgiving and she is relational. She holds space for people to be their most vulnerable. de Haardt explains that "vulnerability and mortality are an inescapable part of life and do not fall outside God's grace" yet "[that] does not alter the fact that the *desire* for healing and wholeness... can be sincere and authentic.... This desire, therefore, is not a denial of vulnerability and mortality; rather a desire for the elimination and liberation of suffering and pain."[93] Anyone can come to Mary with the pain and confusion inherent in human vulnerability and mortality. Mary has a deep compassion which does not deny these difficult truths. For those who practice Marian devotion,

---

[91] de Haardt, "The Marian paradox: Marian practices as a road to a new Mariology?"

[92] de Haardt, "The Marian paradox: Marian practices as a road to a new Mariology?" p. 177.

[93] de Haardt, "The Marian paradox: Marian practices as a road to a new Mariology?" p. 178.

she offers a way to grapple with existential complexities and mitigate pain.

Mary offers an accessible, relatable divinity. She is human like we are human. As Our Lady of Perpetual Help, her love is unconditional and she turns no one away. Marian devotions, in the form of pilgrimages, prayers, lit candles, rosary beads, and images of Mary's likeness offer direct access to her unconditional love. Mary also frequently breaches the boundaries of ordinary consciousness through apparitions which attest to her presence. Mary is present. Her image is available to us. We can approach her through image and tangible action. She is an aspect of the divine who is readily available to those who seek her. de Haardt writes "anyone can turn to Mary, no matter who you are or what you do or believe or whether you believe."[94] She does not deny anyone who seeks her. Her mercy is available to all. This unwavering presence can be immensely healing and uplifting. de Haardt describes Western culture as "predominantly characterized... by 'absence.'"[95] This absence results from widespread alienation from ourselves, each other, and our environments. The concrete actions and images used to connect with Mary, and Mary's unwavering willingness to 'show up' are powerful resistances to this culture of absence. de Haardt emphasizes the importance of Mary's divine presence writing "in the figure of Mary a very specific dimension of the divine, of divine presence, come to the fore: divine presence as unconditional, and precisely on that basis it is a relationship that offers trust and empowerment."[96] While the Church may attempt to employ Mary in service of shaming or repressing women, the lived faith of Marian devotion opens up to the divine presence of Mary, a presence which foregrounds empowerment and unconditional love.

This accessible divine presence also represents access to the divine in feminine form. Our Lady offers an opportunity

---

[94] de Haardt, "The Marian Paradox: Marian practices as a road to a new Mariology?" p. 176.

[95] ibid

[96] ibid

to remember the divine feminine in the context of patriarchal religion. Despite representations of Mary which invoke repressive ideas about women, the practice of Marian devotion continues to emphasize aspects of Mary which are uplifting and empowering. Taylder reminds us of "the ability of women to negotiate and exercise their own agency in the context of patriarchal religious structure."[97] Part of these negotiations involves recognition of divinity in feminine form. Reverence of Mary is reverence of the divine feminine. Taylder describes "Marian devotion as a peculiarly feminine expression of faith."[98] Marian devotion is a practice which often happens in the company of women, drawing on the strength of a feminine divinity. The lived faith of Marian devotion centres feminine images, countering the androcentrism of the Church even while existing within it.

There is a church in Montréal called Notre-Dame-de-Lourdes Chapel. When I first stepped inside, I was stunned. The entire church is a shrine to Mary, with her image repeated over and over again in her many forms. The ceiling has a dome which pictures Mary sitting, feet apart, in a posture of power, depicted as the Queen of Heaven. People come to this church to offer their devotion to her. When I am in this space it impossible for me to deny the living reality of the divine in feminine form, hiding in plain sight within the Catholic Church.

Cunneen writes "Mary's figure was capable of absorbing important aspects of the feminine divine in response to human religious need" and reminds us that "Catholicism managed to preserve part of the old feminine religion in its structure."[99] The divine feminine is preserved through the practice of Marian devotion. Recognizing the divine feminine within the structures of patriarchal Catholicism may seem contradictory. Yet Mary is capable of holding contradiction. According to Cunneen Mary has the "ability to assimilate

---

[97] Taylder, "Our lady of the libido: Towards a Marian Theology of sexual liberation?" p. 358.

[98] Taylder, "Our lady of the libido: Towards a Marian Theology of sexual liberation?" p. 348.

[99] Cunneen, "Breaking Mary's silence: A feminist reflection on Marian piety." p. 330-331.

elements from different cultures, including the pagan."[100] She offers seekers access to an ancient practice of honouring the divine in feminine form.

Along with offering access to the divine feminine, Mary also reminds us of the divinity within materiality. While Catholicism can be described as a transcendent religion organized around a disembodied God, Mary reminds us of the sacredness of the physical. Remembering that the physical is not opposed to the sacred is important, especially for those whose bodies and sexualities have been positioned as shameful or sinful. Mary, like us, is of the flesh. She lived and died, gave birth and breast fed, suffered and felt joy. She was of this world, not apart from it. Her divinity is one which we can access through connection with our bodies. For queer and feminine people whose bodies have been shamed and repressed, Mary can remind us that our bodies are sacred. Living in times of mass environmental destruction, Mary can remind us that this world is sacred.

Christianity promises a heaven beyond this earth and a life beyond our bodies, and these ideas can be used to devalue the physical world and our physical bodies. Mary can act as a corrective to this thinking, pulling us back into our bodies and back into the world. de Haardt writes "the divine is not situated outside of everyday life, which probably nowhere becomes more explicitly clear than in Marian images and devotions."[101] Mary is called by many names; de Haardt lists some of them including "Star of the Sea, Queen of Heaven, Mystical Rose, [and] Seat of Wisdom."[102] Her many names invoke the poetic and metaphoric thinking needed to apprehend Mary in her fullness; they also remind us of the divinity within materiality. de Haardt points out that "Marian titles and symbolism... resonate with references to the divine which can be known in and through the world."[103] Part of Mary's appeal to me as a queer, feminist witch is her

---

[100] Cunneen, "Breaking Mary's silence: A feminist reflection on Marian piety." p. 331.

[101] de Haardt, "The Marian paradox: Marian practices as a road to a new Mariology?" p. 176.

[102] de Haardt, "The Marian paradox: Marian practices as a road to a new Mariology?" p. 177.

[103] ibid

materiality. She calls me back to my body and to the world.

Perhaps most difficult for some people to understand in the invocation of a queer, feminist Marian devotion is how one might discover sexual empowerment, including sexual pleasure, celebrated within the image of the Holy Virgin. The demure, self-effacing, chaste woman of popular Christian imagination does not stir up images of sexual desire. Mary's virginity itself, however we interpret it, may be enough to close the door on considerations of Mary's sexuality. Yet, a queer, feminist engagement with Mary requires that we go deeper, that we suspend our disbelief long enough to catch a glimpse of the Holy Virgin's desire. The scene in the New Testament in which the angel Gabriel tells Mary that she will carry the child of God, called the Annunciation, carries a very important piece of information: Mary's consent. Mary says to the angel Gabriel "Behold the maidservant of the Lord! Let it be to me according to your word."[104] This is important because it highlights Mary's active role in her pregnancy.

Her pregnancy was not something that simply happened to her; it was something that she chose. If we dare to look a little deeper we might also see that the Annunciation reveals Mary's desire. Cunneen quotes a novel by Sara Maitland which explores the role of desire in the Virgin conception.[105] Cunneen quotes Maitland as writing

> [a] purely conscious, unalienated woman who can so assent with the entirety of her person needs no biological intrusion between her desire and its fulfillment. [She is] a slap in the face to anyone who wants to see the virgin birth as anti-sexuality.... sexuality goes beyond the moment of genital reciprocity....She unrooted her desire and carried it as far as it would go; carried it beyond mind and logichigher and higher to the throne of the living God, to the

[104] Luke 1:26-38, New King James Version.

[105] Maitland in Cunneen, "Breaking Mary's silence: A feminist reflection on Marian piety."

source of light, to the infinite word.... Assent becomes the moment of conception.[106]

Maitland's poetic language unchains us from our assumptions and allows us to employ an imaginative, feminist lens in our analysis of Mary. Following Maitland's stunning description, we can imagine Mary's desire as a powerful force. The Virgin birth results from Mary's active, expansive desire. It hinges on her pleasure.

With a creative, feminist approach we can produce a willingness to see Mary's desire. We can revision her story to include space for her pleasure. Our Lady's image has so long been associated with self-denial that it may be difficult, and perhaps seem blasphemous, to remember her pleasure. Yet a queer, feminist Marian devotion carves of space for Mary's complexity. A queer, feminist Marian devotion retrieves aspects of Mary which have been repressed. Honouring the sexuality of the Holy Virgin is a part of this devotion. Her desire and her pleasure are holy in themselves. Taylder writes "[there] is nothing to suggest that Mary did not experience any form of sexual ecstasy and one might be tempted by the notion that such a transcendental event would surely be accompanied by the most exquisite and explosive orgasm."[107] Following Maitland's poetic description of Mary's powerful desire we can easily reach the same conclusion as Taylder.[108] Such powerful desire is likely to result in powerful pleasure.

Taylder invites us to continue in our queer, feminist imaginings by releasing Mary's desire and pleasure from our heteronormative projections, writing "the Annunciation actually subverts patriarchy by replacing the usual male participation with Ruah, the creative spirit of God often experienced in the female inferring that the conception of Jesus was a sexual act from which men were entirely absent."[109] Having remembered Mary's desire, and rediscovered her

---

[106] Cunneen, "Breaking Mary's silence: A feminist reflection on Marian piety." p. 324.

[107] Taylder, "Our lady of the libido: Towards a Marian Theology of sexual liberation?" p. 364.

[108] Cunneen, "Breaking Mary's silence: A feminist reflection on Marian piety."

[109] Taylder, "Our lady of the libido: Towards a Marian Theology of sexual liberation?" p. 364.

pleasure, we can open our minds to her queerness. Mary's pleasure takes place in the context of a nongenital sexual act with a feminine aspect of God. Her pleasure takes place in the context of her enthusiastic consent, her complete assent to this union. Men are absent from this experience. Her pleasure, her desire, turn out to be very queer. Perhaps you feel that we have wandered too far off course by entertaining such queer possibilities, but Taylder reminds us "Nothing is beyond God, certainly not a lesbian conception of Christ."[110]

Mary's likeness hangs above my altar, her Immaculate Heart wreathed and crowned, her gaze steady. At my altar as I light my candles I remember and practice my devotion. Mary's image is misused as an oppressive force in women's lives. Yet I find nothing but comfort and strength in my relationship with her. My queer, feminist, witch heart feels no contradiction with my love for the Queen of Heaven. It feels natural to me to approach Mary with a queer, feminist, imaginative lens. From the moment I found her likeness in the garbage and took her home with me I felt a resonance that allowed me to understand Mary as someone like me.

In my practice of what de Haardt calls "lived faith" I have come to see what Mary can do. She opens herself to me with unconditional love and compassion. She doesn't reject me despite the things I find it hard to accept in myself. As defender of the oppressed, she reminds me of the importance of justice. She casts the mighty from their thrones and lifts up the lowly. As Our Lady of Sorrows, she has room enough to hold space for all my pain. I bring my grief and despair to her, collapse at her feet, and know that there is nothing too big for her to hold. As Our Lady of Mercy her love is unconditional and she welcomes me regardless of how I am feeling aboutmyself. She welcomes the parts of me exiled by society and that parts of me exiled by myself. [111]

As a historical and human woman, she reminds me that my body and this world are divien; she coaxes me to love

---

[110] ibid

[111] de Haardt, "The Marian paradox: Marian practices as a road to a new Mariology?"

my body and this world rather than to escape them. I remember her as I light my candles, as I stop to admire the beauty of the living world. I remember her when I remember my humanness, mortal, imperfect, experiencing both great joy and great sadness. As student Mary guides me in my studies and my writings. She moves me through the procrastination, reminding me of the importance of my word. As the Holy Virgin she reminds me to honour my autonomy and independence. As the Queen of Heaven, she insists on the sacredness of femininity in a world in which femininity is devalued and disrespected. She shows me the divine in feminine form, something that my soul yearns for. With her assent she opens up space for expansive sexual desire and pleasure rooted in active, enthusiastic consent. She shows me what a true complete yes can feel like, what desire can look like unchained from the limits of the heteronormative imaginary.

Mary holds space for all of me, as a queer feminist witch, as a feminine person, as a student, as a seeker of justice, as a human being. Despite the meanings those in power may attach to Mary, if we listen she will speak for herself. Taylder reminds us that "The traditional church and its hierarchies might claim Mary as their own but in truth she belongs to those for whom she remains an integral part of their daily lives."[112] Mary offers herself to the imaginings of those who are devoted to her. A queer feminist Marian devotion is a practice of lived faith.

---

[112] Taylder, "Our lady of the libido: Towards a Marian Theology of sexual liberation?" p. 359.

Trauma Time:

The Queer Temporalities of the Traumatized Mind

There is something very queer about the way I experience time. As a person living with complex trauma, I do not experience time as a straightforward, orderly procession from the past, through the present, to the future. The past rushes up on me with the urgency of the present. The future creeps out of crevices, leaking into the now. The future and past are intimately entwined, the present produced in their merging. Amnesia sucks up whole stories, leaving embodied feelings but no facts. Sections of time are uprooted and relocated into different chapters of my life. The present is disconnected, disoriented, unmapped. My experiences of queer time lead me to theories of queer temporality. Lee Edelman's *No Future: Queer Theory and the Death Drive* proposes a queer anti-futurity which critiques a straight temporality grounded in the future of the symbolic Child.[113] Edelman proclaims "Fuck the social order and the Child in whose name we're collectively terrorized."[114] As a survivor of child abuse whose very queer temporality has been produced through a complete disregard for my safety, Edelman's analysis leaves something to be desired.[115] A proclamation of "Fuck the Child',[116] as José Muñoz,[117] Alison Kafer,[118] and others have pointed out, does not account for the complex lived experiences of actual children.[119]

Along with my discomfort with Edelman's lack of acknowledgment of actual children, and of child abuse as a producer of queer temporalities, is a general awareness of the lack of engagement with disability and madness in the work of Edelman, as well as others theorists of queer temporalities.[120] So, I turned to crip and mad critiques of queer time, in the

---

[113] Edelman, *No future: Queer theory and the death drive.*

[114] Edelman, *No future: Queer theory and the death drive*, p. 29.

[115] ibid

[116] ibid

[117] Muñoz, *Cruising utopia: The then and there of queer futurity.*

[118] Kafer, *Feminist, queer, crip.*

[119] Edelman, *No future: Queer theory and the death drive*, p. 29.

[120] ibid

work of Alison Kafer and Ellen Samuels,[121] and there I was able to find a space in which to begin to think about the queer temporalities of the traumatized mind.[122] After engaging in a recovery of the actual child from the symbol of the Child, and spending some time maddening queer temporalities through crip and mad critiques, I will turn to the queer temporalities of the traumatized mind. I will consider the past as present, amnesia, the present as future as past, and ongoing disorientation in time. Finally, I will turn to Alison Kafer's notion of a "curative imaginary", to consider how trauma, like many disabilities, is framed in relation to hope for a cure.[123] I will propose resisting curative time and embracing the queer time travel of trauma as a means of queer, mad, world-making.

Before considering the queerness of trauma time, I would like to take a moment to recover the actual child from the symbol of the Child, as put forth by Edelman.[124] Edelman argues that the symbol of the Child is the stuff of the future.[125] A heterosexual imaginary projects itself into the future through the symbol of the innocent Child. The Child, as symbol, must therefore be protected at all costs. Edelman writes "the radical right maintains ... the battle against queers is a life-and-death struggle for the future of a Child whose ruin is pursued by feminists, queers, and those who support the legal availability of abortion."[126] This imperative to protect the symbolic child is mobilized politically. Edelman explains "the lives, the speech, and the freedoms of adults face constant threat of legal curtailment out of deference to imaginary Children."[127] While Edelman acknowledges that the Child spoken of here is a symbolic child, rather than a literal one, the lives of actual children are obscured in this

[121] Samuels, *Cripping anti-futurity, or, if you love queer theory so much, why don't you marry it?*

[122] Kafer, *Feminist, queer, crip.*

[123] Kafer, *Feminist, queer, crip*, p. 27.

[124] Edelman, *No future: Queer theory and the death drive.*

[125] ibid

[126] Edelman, *No future*, p. 21-22.

[127] Edelman, *No future*, p. 19.

analysis.[128] Children are, by their very status as children, helpless against domination, exploitation, or neglect from the adults in their lives. They are completely dependent on the care of adults to meet their needs and have no recourse for escape or defense if they are being abused. Real children are not the enemy of queers. The right wing may mobilize the idea of children to further its cause, but children themselves are among those we should struggle in service of. The liberation of all children from domination, exploitation, and abuse, should be included in our struggles for liberation for all oppressed people.

In *Cruising Utopia*, José Muñoz writes "there is... a lot to like in [Edelman's] critique of antireproductive futurism, but ... it is enacted by the active disavowal of a crisis in afrofuturism."[129] Muñoz draws our attention to the fact that the symbolic Child Edelman writes about is implicitly a white child.[130] [131] Racialized children are not afforded the protection imagined as the symbolic implicitly white Child. In reality, racialized children experience racist violence, are dehumanized, and are even murdered due to the racist fantasies of police and other people with guns. In *Feminist, Crip, Queer*, Alison Kafer writes "Edelman's warnings of reproductive futurism, of idealizing the child, read quite differently when they are read alongside 'the lived experiences of ... historical children.'"[132] Kafer goes on to build on Muñoz's important critique writing "[the] always already white Child is also always already healthy and nondisabled; disabled children are not part of this privileged imaginary except as the abject other."[133] [134] Edelman points out that "the cult of the child permits no shrines to the queerness of boys and girls, since queerness... is understood as bringing children and

---

[128] ibid

[129] Muñoz *Cruising utopia*, p. 94.

[130] ibid

[131] Edelman, *No future*.

[132] Kafer, *Feminist, queer, crip*, p. 31-32.

[133] Muñoz *Cruising utopia*.

[134] Kafer, *Feminist, queer, crip*, p. 32-33.

childhood to an end."[135] While the symbolic Child is not imagined as non-white, disabled, or as queer, non-white, disabled, and queer children exist. These children experience the threats and violences of racism, ableism, and homophobia, along with the vulnerability to abuse that all children experience. A theory of queer temporality which proclaims "Fuck the Child" but does not account for real children misses a lot.[136]

Remembering the lived experience of actual children is important. Therefore, it is important for me to acknowledge the reality of child abuse in the lives of so many children. As a survivor of childhood sexual abuse, I can attest to the vast inaction of adults in my life. Besides the person who actively abused me, the other adults in my family failed to protect me and also helped facilitate the abuse by punishing my resistance to it. I shared this information with a number of other adults, including teachers at my school, and nothing happened. I was fifteen by the time anyone reacted to my telling. A social worker I told contacted Children's Aide and the police. Yet, after an investigation, it was decided that there was not enough evidence to press charges or to ensure that my abuser would no longer have access to children. He had access to children until the day he died. Additionally, when I was sixteen, I experienced sexual harassment from a teacher. This same teacher had been accused of having sex with a student, but those accusations were dismissed as gossip. When I attempted to seek help from another teacher, my concerns were framed as stemming from my history of abuse, and as needlessly slandering a teacher's reputation.

These realities of blatant sexual abuse of children, and mass inaction on the part of other adults, and institutions, does not fit Edelmen's declaration that "the lives, the speech, and the freedoms of adults face constant threat of legal curtailment out of deference to imaginary Children."[137] In my

[135] Edelman, No future, p. 19.

[136] Edelman, No future, p. 29.

[137] Edelman, No future, p. 19.

experience actual threat to real children is frequently overlooked in favour of the desires of adults. In fact, I would argue that child abuse is a normative part of the structure of the patriarchal nuclear family, a family structure produced by capitalism, and imposed on colonized peoples through gendered and sexual violence, removal of children from families and imposition of laws which demand colonial gender and family structures. In "Not Murdered, Not Missing: Rebelling Against Colonial Gender Violence" Leanne Betasamosake Simpson writes

> I imagine the colonizers asking ... How do you infuse a society with the heteropatriarchy necessary in order to carry out your capitalist dreams when Indigenous men aren't actively engaged in upholding a system designed to exploit women? ... the introduction of gender violence is one answer. Destroying and then reconstructing sexuality and gender identity is another. Residential schools did an excellent job on both accounts.[138]

I suggest that straight time as a capitalist construct is in many ways dependent on child abuse and gendered violence, even as it uses the symbol of the Child to represent its future. So, while Edelman proposes a queer anti-futurity which abandons the symbolic Child, the actual children who experience child abuse are not addressed.[139] I find this especially troublesome because it is my experience of childhood sexual abuse, and the ensuing trauma, which produced my own queer temporalities. Rather than an anti-futurity and a 'fuck the child' stance, I propose a queer time traveling, which makes space for mad and crip embodiments.

Remembering child abuse, and trauma, in discussions of queer temporalities is important to me, because it is my embodied experience of trauma which queers time. Trauma

---

[138] Simpson, "Not murdered, not missing," para. 19.

[139] Edelman, *No future.*

is what allows me to understand time as queer, as something that does not follow a straight trajectory. Yet, when I sat down to research this paper, I discovered that trauma, and other experiences of disability, are curiously missing in much of the theorizing on queer temporalities. In order to madden, and crip, queer temporality, we have to draw our attention to what is present but made absent through lack of engagement. It was here that I turned to the work of Ellen Samuels and Alison Kafer for crip critiques of queer temporality.[140]

In "Cripping Anti-Futurity, or, If You Love Queer Theory So Much, Why Don't You Marry It?" Ellen Samuels takes up the work of Jack Halberstam, Lee Edelman and other theorists of queer temporality, writing "it seems … that the complicated and impassioned discussions of queer temporalities and queer futurity in the past several years have proceeded as if people with disabilities, queer or otherwise, do not exist."[141] Samuels takes issue with the simultaneous presence and absence of disability in these texts, noting that while the queer temporalities of illness, unemployment, and interdependence are foundational to theories of queer temporalities, disability itself is never named.[142]

Samuel goes on to say "the ill and suffering, marginalized and abjected, dependent and interdependent bodies which populate [these] books and often provide the most compelling examples of queer temporality are at once essential and unnamed, foregrounded and made invisible."[143] Alison Kafer in Queer, Feminist, Crip also notices and takes issue with the simultaneous glaring absence and presence of disability within theories of queer temporalities, noting that while disability is not named outright, it is disability which underpins these theories.[144] Kafer writes "[one] could argue

---

[140] Samuels, *Cripping anti-futurity, or, if you love queer theory so much, why don't you marry it?* and Kafer, *Feminist, queer, crip.*

[141] Samuels, *Cripping anti-futurity, or, if you love queer theory so much, why don't you marry it?* p. 4.

[142] ibid

[143] Samuels, *Cripping anti-futurity, or, if you love queer theory so much, why don't you marry it?* p. 5.

[144] Kafer, *Feminist, queer, crip.*

that queer time *is* crip time, and that it has been all along. Queer time is often defined through or in reference to illness and disability, suggesting that it is illness and disability that render time "queer."[145] I join with Samuels and Kafer in explicitly reinserting disability into theories of queer temporalities. In this case, I offer trauma time as a maddening of queer time.[146]

A major component of trauma is a re-experiencing of the past with the visceral intensity of the present. Flashbacks can include any combination of the senses, including intense visual, auditory, olfactory, and tactile recreations of a traumatic experience. Flashbacks are different from regular memories because the body experiences them as if they are happening in the present, producing a stress response intended for emergencies. The emergency happened in the past, but the response is happening in the present. In "Trauma and Temporality," Robert Stolorow writes "[experiences] of trauma become freeze-framed into an eternal present in which one remains forever trapped, or to which one is condemned to be perpetually returned...."[147] Nightmares, like flashbacks, transform the past into a visceral present. Trauma survivors often experience intense nightmare reenacting aspects of traumatic events. I have awoken in terror standing up, and I have also been awoken by my own terrified voice speaking out loud. The intensity of my flashbacks and nightmares overrides the present, replacing it with a past that seems far more real. Intrusive thoughts can also be an experience of past as present, hearing the voices of abusers, or responses to abusers that were never vocalized, playing over and over on a loop.

Amnesia is another way that trauma queers time. This can take the form of complete forgetting, partial forgetting, body memories and structural dissociation. Trauma can cause complete memories to be blocked from consciousness,

---

[145] Kafer, *Feminist, queer, crip* p. 34.

[146] Samuels, *Cripping anti-futurity, or, if you love queer theory so much, why don't you marry it?* and Kafer, *Feminist, queer, crip*

[147] Stolorow, "Trauma and temporality," p. 160.

or memories may be available only partially. There are some traumatic experiences which I remember most of, but a particular aspect is just a gaping hole, implied by the surrounding context, but unavailable to my conscious mind. Memories can also include sensations, images, sounds, but not include an overarching narrative. This causes difficulty in legal contexts where survivors are expected to produce orderly, linear accounts of the violence that they experienced.

In "Transforming Past Agency and Action in the Present" Paula Reavey and Steven D. Brown explain that the narration of trauma within the legal contexts "acquire[s] a discrete and determinate character" and in other contexts "the same past experience might be configured and extracted in a less determinate form."[148] I have gone through a rape trial, and my rapist's defense lawyer asked me temporal questions about the exact order of events, the location of the rape within the timeline of my relationship with my abuser, and the length of the rape itself. These questions attempt to force my traumatized relationship to time into a linear telling. Like many survivors, I was unable to provide answers which satisfied the defense lawyer's linear logics, and this acted against my credibility.

Trauma can be remembered and forgotten simultaneously, through body memories and also through structural dissociation. In the case of body memories, pain, an intense reaction to a particular type of touch, and other embodied experiences, can take the place of narrative memories. In the case of structural dissociation, the personality can be split so that one part of the personality remembers, and another does not. Dissociated aspects of the personality can have entirely different versions of a life narrative.

Hypervigilance and avoidance are practices of attempting to prevent future trauma by looking for signs of past trauma in the present. Kafer writes

---

[148] Reavey and Brown, "Transforming past agency and action in the present time, social remembering, and child sexual abuse," p. 190.

'Strange temporalities' could … include the experiences of those with PTSD … who live in a kind of anticipatory time, scanning their days for events or exposures that might trigger a response. Such scans include moving both forward and backward in time while remaining present in this moment.[149]

Hypervigilance and avoidance are a mapping of the past onto the present in order to avoid a particular future which could recreate a traumatic past. Scanning the environment for potential threats, avoiding situations which could be threatening or which remind of the original trauma, these are temporal practices which are about the past as much as the future, and yet they shape the present.

The final aspect of trauma's queer temporality I will explore here, though this is not an exhaustive exploration, is ongoing disorientation in time. This can include dissociation, executive dysfunction, and confusion. Trauma survivors often have difficulty with organization, planning, prioritizing, scheduling, and other temporal tasks. Trauma survivors often experience dissociation, derealization, and depersonalization, experiences which can feel like being 'outside' of time, and even reality. I have found myself at the right location, at the right time, on the wrong day. This ongoing confusion and disorientation in relation to time exemplifies the queerness of trauma time. I may suddenly remember in exact detail a traumatic event that happened years ago, or be caught up in the minute work of projecting past terrors onto potential futures, but if I am asked what I did yesterday, or what I am doing on the weekend, I am often left perplexed. Time, for me, does not function as a matter-of-fact linear procession. It is more like a complex, dynamic web of information and experience in which I can move in any direction, and, in which I am frequently lost.

---

[149] Kafer, *Feminist, queer, crip*, p. 38

The queer temporalities of my traumatized mind are not a problem, a tragedy, or an unfortunate condition requiring a cure. Some of these experiences are stressful, difficult, or distressing. I may choose to do work to ground myself in the present, to integrate my personality, to let go of hypervigilance, to return to the safety of now. But my queer temporalities are also a different way of being in the world, a creative, flexible, and nonlinear way of relating to time. They offer insights, possibilities, and perspectives that I would not have if I only understood time chronologically. While my experience of time was queered by violence, that does not mean that my resulting lived, embodied experience of the world is bad or wrong. I suggest that my experience of queer temporalities opens up possibilities for different ways of being in the world, and refutes the apparently objective naturalness of linear time. Yet most representations of the embodied experience of trauma position it as an undesirable way of being, in need of a cure.

This brings me to Kafer's notion of a "curative imaginary."[150] The curative imaginary refers to the way that experiences of disability are temporally framed in relation to a future, potential cure. Kafer uses 'curative' rather than 'cure' to indicate that the problem is a compulsory orientation toward cure, not the various feelings or desires which individual disabled people may have in relation to the possibility of a cure.[151] Kafer is critiquing "an understanding of disability that not only *expects* and *assumes* intervention but also cannot imagine or comprehend anything other than intervention."[152] I was once speaking to someone about my experiences with dissociation. I was told that I should resist dissociation at all costs because engaging in it was worsening my condition. The underlying message is that I should strive to have a normative relationship to time.

---

[150] ibid

[151] ibid

[152] Kafer, *Feminist, queer, crip*, p. 27.

I do not have a normative relationship to time. The way that I experience time is very queer. I cannot easily place myself in the here and now, nor do I understand the here and now as having a straightforward relationship to the past or the future. The past can overtake my present. The future can move backwards into the past. Memories can exist on different timelines or can fail to exist at all. Time is a disorienting and confusing place, but mainly because I am expected to relate to it in particular ways. I have started the practice of replying to the small talk question *What did you do this weekend?* with the honest answer of *I don't know.* People look perplexed when I say this because they are expecting that I have a straight forward relationship to the immediate past. I do not. In fact, there is nothing straight about my relationship to the past, present, or future, as I do not experience them as distinct entities with predictable causal relationships.

While I admit that flashbacks are exhausting, nightmares are horrifying, dissociation can be uncomfortable, disorientation can be confusing, and hypervigilance can be extremely inconvenient, I also must assert that I love my embodied experience of queer trauma time. Like Kafer asserts, I can have particular desires about healing aspects of my traumatized subjectivity while still valuing and enjoying other aspects of it. Not being attached to linear, normative time has produced a flexible, imaginative way of being in the world. I think so much of my creativity capacity as a writer is due to the way that I wander through time. I also see my queer experience of time as connected to my drive toward liberation. By moving fluidly through the past, present, and future I can carry messages through time. I can bring lessons from the past into the present, and lessons from the future into the past. I experience the time travel of trauma as a call for justice, as motivation to produce futures which are not repetitions of traumatic past, and as motivation for world-building that values difference. The queer time travel of trauma can be a means of queer, mad, world-making. Rather than an anti-futurity which proclaims 'fuck the child', the queer temporalities of trauma time seek justice for children, and other survivors of violence, while creatively and imaginatively finding ways to survive and thrive in a violent world. The queer time travel of trauma resists linearity and causality as the only right, or natural ways to relate to time, and instead opens up time as a space that can be moved through in any direction, affirming the pain of violent pasts, and dreaming of just futures.

Intoxication Spaces:

Mental Maps

of

Substance Use

(Part One)

Space is not natural or neutral. It is designed and mapped in particular ways. These dominant maps are shaped by systems of power like capitalism, colonialism, racism, ableism, homophobia, and misogyny. These dominant maps attempt to shape and control the way that space is used and who can use it. Superimposed onto these dominant maps are the mental maps of people who use space. These mental maps can reinforce the dominant maps by re-inscribing the intended use of space. They can also resist, subvert or undermine the dominant map by creating new meanings and uses of spaces.

Intoxication culture is a dominant culture which produces a particular standard of substance use, social drinking, as a norm which people are then expected to live up to. Intoxication culture has its dominant maps which shape space in order to encourage social drinking, and exclude or punish non-normative relationships to substances such as active addiction, specific forms of drug use, and sobriety. The dominant maps of intoxication culture work with capitalism to be especially punitive toward homeless people, and others who use drugs and drink in criminalized and street involved ways. Reflecting on my own history of active addiction and current sobriety, I note how two very different mental maps are produced, and how these maps differ from the dominant map of intoxication culture. The mental maps of non-normative substance users are superimposed over the dominant map of intoxication culture, revealing that our relationships to substance use shape our relationships to space.

In the introduction to *Race, Space and The Law*, entitled "When Place Becomes Race" Sherene Razack suggests that we can "reject the view that spaces simply evolve, are filled up with things, and exist either prior to or separate from the subjects who imagine and use them."[153] Rather than understanding space as natural and neutral, Razack suggests that space should be understood, in Lefebvre's terms, as "perceived, conceived and lived."[154] Thinking of space as

---

[153] Razack, "When place becomes race," p. 8.

[154] Razack, "When place becomes race," p. 9.

perceived allows us to consider the everyday uses and practices which shape space. Understanding space as conceived allows us to think of space as intentionally designed by planners, architects, corporations, and governments. Reflecting on space as lived allows us to consider the ways that users of space interpret the perceived and conceived uses of space in order to create meanings of space. Razack's analysis of space helps us to understand that space is not simply 'there' but is created through intentional design, everyday practice, interpretation and representation.[155] Space is conceived in the interests of capitalism and other systems of power. Users of space interact with the conceived or intended uses of space, perceiving space in their own ways and living their own meanings of space into being. These meanings can reinforce, undermine, resist or confirm the intended use of space as it was conceived.

In "Narratives of Place: Subjective and Collective" Gordon Brent Ingram, Anne-Marie Bouthillette and Yolanda Retter suggest that "there are maps that report the physical geography of a landscape and more subjective maps that exist 'in our heads.'"[156] Following Razack, I argue that the maps which report the physical geography are no more objective than the maps which exist 'in our heads.' Physical geography, as Razack explains, is conceived in particular ways.[157] It is useful, however, to note the differences between these dominant maps and the mental maps which exist 'in our heads.' Mental maps map what Razack refers to as lived space.[158] They are maps which vary from person to person, though members of particular communities and social locations will experience similarities in their mental maps. These maps lay out the ways in which users of space navigate and negotiate with the dominant maps. Ingram, Bouthillette and Retter write "[each] person's 'map' is usually part autobiography, part

---

[155] ibid

[156] Ingram, Bouthillette, and Retter, "Narratives of place: Subjective and collective," p. 55.

[157] Razack, "When place becomes race."

[158] ibid

mythology, and part the embodiment of tensions concerning forms of marginality, such as sexual politics, gender, race, ethnicity, or culture."[159] Mental maps allow us to understand how the same space may be experienced entirely differently by different people. They reveal "'differential cognition' of the same places and different 'affinities.'"[160]

Dominant maps set out the conceived and intended uses of space. Within intoxication culture, space is conceived in particular ways with relation to substance use. In *Towards A Less Fucked Up World: Sobriety and Anarchist Struggles* Nikita Riotfag defines intoxication culture as "a set of institutions, behaviours, and mindsets centered around consumption of drugs and alcohol."[161] Intoxication culture is a culture in which people are expected to partake in a particular type of substance use, social drinking, and are excluded or punished for other relationships to substances such as active addiction, certain types of drugs use, or sobriety. The standard of normative consumption, and the construction of non-normative consumption, will shift and change depending on context and social location. For example, drinking to the point of drunkenness is acceptable on a Friday or Saturday night but not on a Tuesday morning. Also, white or middle class youth drinking in a park might receive a warning from police while racialized or street involved youth may experience criminal charges, incarceration, or police violence for the same activity. A joint may be acceptable to pass around at a party and still be considered normative consumption, a crack pipe would not. The shifting construction of 'normative consumption' produces different mental maps of spaces of intoxication. The dominant map of intoxication culture is a map which privileges middle class people and criminalizes the same behavior for racialized, street involved, or homeless people.

While walking in the Queen Street West neighborhood

---

[159] Ingram, et al "Narratives of place: Subjective and collective," p. 56.

[160] Ingram et al, "Narratives of place: Subjective and collective," p. 59.

[161] Riotfag, *Towards a less fucked up world: Sobriety and anarchist struggle,* p. 4.

and thinking through the intersections of space, mental mapping and intoxication culture, I am struck by my awareness of two overlapping mental maps. Currently, it is day time and I am using the space as it is designed to be used. I am running errands, shopping, engaging in capitalist consumption. I engage with the space as it is mapped. I hurry past crowds of window shoppers, moving from store to store to spend money. Yet, out of the corner of my eye, I am aware of another map. Years ago, I used this same space for very different purposes. During my years of active alcoholism, this space carried different meanings and had a different mental map. Markers on my alcoholic mental map of Queen Street West included: coffee shops that let me use the washroom without buying anything, alleyways I could get away with pissing in, good and contested spots for panhandling, likely places to pick up weed, parks where the police frequented, parks where the police were less likely to come by, places to pass out where I was more or less likely to be sexually assaulted, the 'sally van' spot where we could access free food, bars I was banned from though I didn't usually drink in bars, and of course, the Wine Rack, the Beer Store and the nearest LCBO.

This mental map of my alcoholic use of the space is not the intended or sanctioned map. At the same time, my alcoholic mental map is not the only mental map of non-normative substance use. My alcoholic mental map is shaped by my social locations: my whiteness shaped my interactions with police, my experience of being read as a woman means that my alcoholic mental map includes consideration of sexual violence, my position as a street involved alcoholic with mental health issues produces a different alcoholic mental map than that of an alcoholic who drinks in the clubs or bars of the area. Now that I am three and a half years sober, I no longer use my alcoholic mental map, but it remains in my mind, superimposed over this sanctioned map of capitalist consumption.

Failure

to

Comply:

Madness as

Testimony

Self-harm, suicide attempts, disordered eating, addiction, and other forms of "acting out" are associated with the trauma of surviving violence. While these behaviours are pathologized as symptoms of mental illness, they can be understood, instead, as strategies of resistance against violence. When violence is ignored or normalized, the "acting out" associated with trauma can be a means of sounding an alarm that something is very wrong. This "acting out" can be understood as an embodied form of testimony. When direct resistance to violence, such as fighting back or escaping, is thwarted or impossible, traumatic "acting out" can be a way to draw attention to and resist violence. Psychiatry, instead of answering the call of trauma by addressing the underlying violence, works to silence that call.

Through incarceration, sexual violence, enforced isolation, restricted motion, threats, coercive drugging, gaslighting, and other abusive tactics, psychiatry works to undermine the embodied testimony of trauma by producing compliance. The source of the problem is shifted from the original violence and located instead in the body of the traumatized person. Successful treatment is understood as the reduction or elimination of the very "symptoms" which are in reality acts of resistance to violence. Therefore, successful treatment essentially means submission. The carceral space of psychiatry continues the work of producing compliance even after the patient has left its enclosures, extending the space of the psych ward into the everyday lives of psychiatric survivors.

I make these arguments largely based on my lived experience as a psychiatric survivor. This essay makes the methodological move of mapping madness in its encounters with incarceration and choosing to centre my own, firsthand, embodied accounts of psychiatrization. Joining a long history of psychiatric survivor testimony, I offer my experiences as a call to action against the institutionalized violence of psychiatry. Mark Cresswell, while tracing the history of psychiatric and self-harm survivor self-advocacy and testimony in the UK, writes "[if] self-advocacy is the form that survivor-activism takes, then "direct experience" is the well of knowledge from which it draws."[162] I draw from the well of my lived experience with madness and psychiatry in order to invoke in the reader the sense of violation that I have lived.

Cresswell reminds us that the impact of psychiatric survivor testimony is "affective, but also visceral and not just cognitive; it is not the same as... the presentation of third person vignettes."[163] I offer my firsthand, embodied experiences in the hopes of invoking an affective, visceral response. Ultimately, I hope that this affective, visceral telling produces within the reader a call to action. Creswell writes, "testimony aims to bring into being a state of affairs in which the survivor's truth is witnessed as an event about which 'something ought to be done.'"[164] In writing this testimony, I join a rich history of psychiatric survivors and mad-identified people who collectively draw on the well of our lived experiences in order to draw attention to realities about which something ought to be done.

Shaindl Diamond, in a critical ethnography of Toronto's overlapping communities of psychiatrized people, discerns three ideological frameworks present in these communities. Diamond calls these frameworks "constituencies"[165] and names them the psychiatric survivor constituency, the mad constituency, and the antipsychiatry constituency.[166] While these constituencies are by no means discrete or exhaustive of the approaches within psychiatrized communities, Diamond's analysis offers important tools for thinking through the activism and community building of psychiatrized people.

According to Diamond, the psychiatric survivor constituency focuses on the violence of psychiatry, drawing on the testimony of psychiatric survivors and offering peer-led community support. The mad constituency focuses on

---

[162] Cresswell, "Psychiatric "survivors" and testimonies of self-harm," p. 1671

[163] Cresswell, "Psychiatric "survivors" and testimonies of self-harm," p. 1674.

[164] Cresswell, "Psychiatric "survivors" and testimonies of self-harm," p. 1672.

[165] Diamond, "What makes ss a community?"

[166] ibid

mad identity, remaining critical of psychiatry but shifting the focus from psychiatry onto mad people themselves. The antipsychiatry constituency draws on the lived experience of psychiatric survivors, but also includes the perspectives of academics and professionals who are not psychiatric survivors, with the aim of abolishing psychiatry entirely.

Diamond offers important suggestions for building community and solidarity among these overlapping and divergent perspectives. Each of these constituencies draws on psychiatric survivor testimony as a strategy in varying ways. The psychiatric survivor constituency relies on survivor testimony most exclusively and frequently, the mad constituency uses survivor testimony but also employs narratives of madness, and the antipsychiatry constituency draws on survivor testimony as well as analysis by non-survivors. While I have affinities with each of these frameworks, I locate myself and this work within the psychiatric survivor framework. I am most interested in producing testimony that reveals the violence of psychiatry and functions as a call to action toward a more just world.

Along with functioning as a call to action, psychiatric survivor testimony can function as a form of solidarity and community building. It can be the whisper that says, "it happened to me too." I first came to stories of madness and surviving psychiatry through zines. These were zines that talked about surviving incest, self-harm, and getting locked up. I don't remember the names or authors of the zines I came across in my teenage years, but I remember their message. I didn't need to be convinced of the reality of the violence that these writers faced, but their words helped convince me of the reality of the violence that I faced. I no longer felt completely alone. I had the company of strangers who confirmed for me that I was not crazy to believe that what happened to me was wrong. I started writing zines myself, and while this essay situates itself within mad studies scholarship, it ultimately draws on a lineage with its roots outside the academy. I write for the psychiatric survivors who were brave enough to tell their stories and for those who are just beginning to find words for what happened or is happening. In her memoir *Dirty River*, long-time zinester, poet, and author Leah Lakshmi Piepzna-Samarasinha writes about discovering the mad movement through zines and then finding psychiatric survivor community in Toronto.[167] She writes:

> I hadn't been drugged or shocked or locked up, but I lived my life constantly worried that I would be. I just hadn't been caught yet. I was like the others, even if I wasn't in the psych hospital. The protests were important. But what was even more important was the compassion. Just the room to be crazy.[168]

Psychiatric survivor testimony creates room to be crazy. It opens up space in which other survivors might dare to speak. It offers witness and validation by declaring that this violence happened to me too. Psychiatric survivor testimony is a powerful claim to the truth in the face of a silencing violence. I offer this article as another voice in this lineage of survivor stories.

Self-harm and other forms of "acting out" associated with trauma function as a form of testimony in and of themselves. Psychiatric survivors use testimony, written or spoken accounts of lived experience with psychiatry, in order to draw attention to and to resist the institutionalized violence of psychiatry. Testimony contests the hegemony of psychiatry by offering survivor knowledges as alternative claims to truth.[169] This strategy within mad movements echoes the strategy of self-harm and other forms of "acting out" associated with trauma: both function as testimony and alternative claims to truth.

While I grew up experiencing sexual abuse, the dominant narrative within my family was that nothing

---

[167] Piepzna-Samarasinha, *Dirty river.*

[168] Piepzna-Samarasinha, *Dirty river*, p. 150.

[169] Cresswell, "Psychiatric "survivors" and testimonies of self-harm."

unusual or violent was going on. My cutting functioned as testimony to the reality of the violence that I experienced. It was a claim to the truth. Psychiatry worked to silence this testimony and its implicit call to action. The violence that I experienced was not addressed but the "symptom" of my cutting was silenced through coercion. By joining with other psychiatric survivors in the strategy of testimony, I reclaim the meaning of my self-harm, restoring it to its original function of testimony in and of itself. The resonance between self-harm and testimony as strategies highlights the importance of acting as witnesses and responding when we are called to action.

Self-Harm and/as Testimony

I have been feeling more and more like I don't exist. There is this strange sensation that I have dematerialized. There is the rising of unbearable pressure, something worse than melancholy and far more urgent. I have been having breakdowns at school. Falling down in the middle of the hallway, pulling at my hair, wrapping my body up into a ball. It feels like something must be done but I don't know what. Today I took all the Tylenol that was left in the bottle. I know it wasn't enough to die but I feel stoned and sick. I wander the halls telling people I have a headache and asking if they have anything I can take. I manage to get more pills this way. By lunch I've realized this might have been a bad idea so I eat something hoping it will absorb the poison of overdose. At last period I ask my friend if she will skip class with me. She says she has to go to class. We separate and I continue to wander the halls. Later, I find her leaving the school with her boyfriend. Something snaps in me. The building pressure has risen past the point of containment, even the sick haze of overdose can't keep it at bay. I move quickly, urgently, the certainty of my actions suddenly, automatically clear. I reach into a recycling bin, find a clear glass bottle, leave the school in a rush, cross the parking lot. I can hear my friend calling my name but she is in another world, a world I don't belong to. At the other side of the parking lot I kneel and smash the bottle. I collect the shards in the palm of my hand. I leave the school property and walk several blocks before stopping somewhere at the side of the road. There is a large truck parked there, the shadow of which offers me enough privacy. On the grass, I select a shard and take it to the skin on the inside of my arm. I find a way to make the cut; the blood releases. As quickly as I can, in desperate need of this relief, I slash my arms over and over again. Time has stopped. Everything has stopped. All there is, is glass and blood and pain.

When I was 15 years old, I began cutting myself, overdosing on pills, and having episodes in the middle of my high school. The above vignette illustrates one such episode, one that ended up having a profound impact on the course of my life. There were many such episodes. There was also the visible crisscrossing of scabbed over cuts covering the surface of my arms. I hid my cuts at home but I allowed them to be visible at school. Some students approached the staff about this, and I was made to see the school social worker.

During one of our sessions, I mentioned my stress over having to visit my grandparents because my grandfather made sexual comments about the children in my family and had forcibly made out with me when I was 12. I relayed this information casually. I did not understand this to be "my problem," the reason I was cutting and overdosing, or even a big deal. My family made it clear that my grandfather's behaviour was acceptable and normal, and that if I resisted I was rude and ungrateful. So I was shocked when the social worker called Children's Aid and the police. This didn't end the abuse in my life, but it did mean that I never had to see my grandfather again.

To most people the overdosing, the cutting, and the episodes that I was having at school appeared to be spontaneous, erratic behaviour. Those who had sympathy for me understood me as sick and in need of help. Those who did not understood me as selfish, irresponsible, and attention-seeking. My embodied experience of my behaviour, as expressed in the above vignette, was not linked to the abuse. I understood my behaviour as a pressing, urgent reaction to extreme physical and emotional discomfort. As someone who was experiencing ongoing sexual abuse and who was being told that nothing out of the ordinary was actually happening, my traumatic "acting out" was a means of making visible the violence that I was experiencing. Though I was not consciously aware of my reasoning, my self-harm functioned as a strategy of resistance. My cuts produced an alternate claim to truth from that of my parents. My cuts declared visibly that something was very wrong and bore witness to "an event about which 'something ought to be done.'"[170] In this case, my strategy of resistance was successful in that my self-harm directly resulted in me never having to see an adult who was abusing me again.

Despite the obvious reasons for my distress, my traumatic "acting out" was psychiatrized and eventually resulted in my incarceration in a psychiatric institution. Instead of acknowledgment that my behaviour was in fact an effective strategy against violence, my "acting out" was responded to with further violence. Instead of receiving the support and care that I needed to recover from the trauma of sexual abuse, I was treated as a problem in need of a solution. The location of the problem was shifted from the adults who abused and neglected me to my own body as a chemically imbalanced site of disorder.

Erick Fabris and Katie Aubrecht explain that "Psychiatric prescriptions make it possible to define social suffering and dissent as signs or symptoms of the existence of personal disorder and moral weakness, rather than embodied responses to inequitable social systems."[171] My suffering and my dissent were used against me as signs of sickness. Given the lack of power that I had as a child experiencing abuse from my caregivers, I am struck by my resourcefulness in communicating my suffering and dissent. Having no means to protect myself or to escape my situation, my traumatic "acting out" was an effective strategy for calling attention to and resisting the violence that was happening to me. Yet,

---

[170] Cresswell, "Psychiatric "survivors" and testimonies of self-harm," p. 1672.

[171] Fabris & Aubrecht, "Chemical Constraint: Experiences of psychiatric coercion, restraint, and detention as carceratory techniques," p. 187.

this very resourcefulness was deemed the problem and used to justify further violence.

The psychiatric response to self-harm is to put an end to it, resorting to incarceration and forced medication if necessary. This is a refusal to answer the call of the testimony that self-harm offers. Instead of responding to self-harm with compassion and concern, psychiatry works to silence those who self-injure. By the time I resorted to cutting myself, I had already experienced years of sexual abuse that was ignored or facilitated by the adults in my life. I had disclosed the sexual assault to my parents and to other adults to no avail. I was forced to accept my parents' version of reality, which presented the sexual abuse as normal and acceptable. Yet I could not accept this version of reality because I lived in utter terror.

Self-harm gave voice to my violation. The unbearable pressure of living the unlivable was relieved as my body bore witness to the reality of the violence that I was subjected to. As Cresswell writes:

> A growing number of *women* are choosing to call themselves "survivors" because they are *driven to self harm* by a society that *violates them as children and adults, ignores their personal experiences,* then compounds the violation within an ostensibly *helping system that actually harms them*. [172]

I was driven to self-harm as a last resort against the violence that I was experiencing. My self-harm was then used to justify my incarceration. The day that I took a glass bottle out of the recycling bin and cut my arms on the side of the road was the day that landed me in a locked psychiatric unit for the first time. My behaviour told a story of a child who was enduring something terrible. Yet the response was to treat me as mentally ill, to take away my freedom, and to silence the testimony of my self-harm through coercion and force.

---

[172] Cresswell, "Psychiatric "survivors" and testimonies of self-harm," p. 1675, emphasis in original.

Psychiatry and/as Sexual Violence

After the trip to the emergency room and the drinking of liquid charcoal, I am told that this episode represents a major departure from anything I have done before. The hospital has made a referral to a locked psychiatric unit in downtown Toronto. The following day my parents drive me from my hometown. Upon arriving at the Youthdale Secure Treatment Centre I am separated from my parents. After answering a series of questions I am led into a small room with a shower. I am handed two small paper cups. The woman staff member I have just met explains that one has shampoo and the other has soap. I am told to undress and to place my clothing and glasses in a plastic bin. I am told to shower and wash my hair. I do so quickly as the woman waits outside the shower. I am told to step out of the shower. I stand there naked, soaking wet and unable to see because I don't have my glasses. The staff member looks me over, tells me to turn around and then looks me over some more. She hands me a tiny towel, a pair of oversized gray sweatpants and an oversized gray sweatshirt. She tells me to get dressed and to wait. She leaves with my clothes and glasses. I dry myself with the towel as best I can and put on the clothing. She returns and instructs me to follow her. I am disoriented without my glasses. My hair is dripping wet. I am wearing strange, wrong fitting clothing. I am in shock from being made, without warning or explanation, to present my naked 15-year-old body to another person for the first time since I was a young child. In this state, I am brought into the unit.

Arriving at the locked facility in Toronto was shocking in and of itself. I had no idea what to expect. Being immediately separated from my parents and ushered into the shower room with little explanation was overwhelming to say the least. I was utterly unprepared for the experience of being made to shower and stand naked in front of a stranger. The fact that I was already a survivor of sexual violence made this encounter particularly traumatizing. This violation was justified as being for my own protection. The need to survey my naked, wet body was framed as a search for objects that I might use to harm myself. Even then, I understood the act as an invasion of my privacy and degradation of my personhood. I now understand this act as sexual violence.

In the book *Are Prisons Obsolete?* Angela Y. Davis quotes Amanda George:

> The acknowledgement that sexual assault does occur in institutions for people with intellectual disabilities, prisons, psychiatric hospitals, youth training centres and police stations, usually centres around the criminal acts of rape and sexual assault by individuals employed in those institutions. These offences, though they are rarely reported, are clearly understood as being 'crimes' for which the individual and not the state is responsible. At the same time as the state deplores 'unlawful' sexual assaults by its employees, it actually uses sexual assault as a means of control. …prison and police officers are vested with the power and responsibility to do acts which, if done outside of work hours, would be crimes of sexual assault.[173]

Sexual violence is carried out routinely. It is not framed as violence but as procedure. My consent was not required. My history of sexual trauma was not considered. This traumatizing experience made clear to me that within the walls of the psychiatric hospital I had no power.

Sexual violence is a tool used to produce compliance. Being made to shower and stand naked while being inspected by a stranger, being made to wear wrong fitting clothing that was not my own, along with the confiscation of my glasses, worked together to strip me of my personhood, demean me, and disorient me. It compounded the existing sexual trauma that led to me ending up in the psychiatric hospital in the first place. This violence in no way contributed to my healing or wellness. Forcing a child who has survived sexual abuse to strip naked in front of a stranger was not done in the name of healing. Rather, it worked to re-traumatize me and to remove

---

[173] Davis, *Are prisons obsolete?* p. 82

my ability to resist. As Davis points out, this kind of violence functions as a "means of control": reducing me to a state of traumatization, taking personal clothing that would have reminded me of who I was, and taking away my glasses so that I was unable to see effectively, all worked to take away my power.[174] This was done to me immediately upon arrival and before entering into the locked unit so that I entered the unit in a state of powerlessness.

The Youthdale Secure Treatment Centre's website claims that their "goal is to help children express their feelings appropriately, understand the relationship between emotions, thoughts, and actions, and learn to control their harmful behaviour."[175] Despite claiming to provide a "structured and safe therapeutic environment"[176], the focus remains on the child's "harmful behaviour." [177] It is this "harmful behaviour" that I argue functions as testimony and resistance to violence. This "harmful behaviour"works to make visible suffering and dissent.

My cutting was a desperate attempt to survive and draw attention to sexual violence. This was responded to by subjecting me to further sexual violence. The goal of the Youthdale Secure Treatment Centre, and psychiatry more generally, is not healing or wellness. Rather, despite the use of words like "safe" and "therapeutic," words which my experience reveals to be untrue, the goal is clearly control. This word remains in their description along with their attempts to hide and soften the means through which they achieve that control, means which includesexual violence. I suggest that the "harmful behaviour" which requires control is not the self-harm of a traumatized child, but the routine use of sexual violence within psychiarty as a means to produce

---

[174] ibid

[175] Youthdale Treatment Centres, "Secure treatment to help children in a safe environment," para. 3.

[176] Youthdale Treatment Centres, "Secure treatment to help children in a safe environment," para. 4.

[177] Youthdale Treatment Centres, "Secure treatment to help children in a safe environment," para.3.

compliance.

Isolation and/as Immobilization

At meals they always seat us with patients most unlike ourselves. I am never permitted to sit near the other teenage girls. Talking, beyond the basics of passing the juice, is not permitted. Seating us with the people we are least likely to talk to is meant to help facilitate this. I share a small table with three young boys, all of them probably under thirteen years old. The boy sitting next to me, a lively, friendly child of maybe eight years old, announces that he doesn't like spaghetti and he doesn't want to eat it. This, a perfectly normal statement from a child his age, fills the room with tension. No one says anything. A staff member explains to him that he has to eat it, and if he doesn't, he won't get a snack before bed. The nighttime snacks of packaged cookies are, for most of us, a highly prized aspect of mainly silent, mostly unpleasant days. The boy is visibly upset. He begins to argue. He begins to cry. He begins to raise his voice. He is warned one more time and then he is taken away. Away to wherever they take patients when they do not behave, away to where the cries and screams abruptly stop, and they are not seen again for days.

Fabris and Aubrecht write, "psychiatry's premise of reordering or curing identity (the disorderly 'mad' body) leads to the apparent intent to immobilize it first, then to treat it."[178] The authors explore the ways in which psychiatric drugs are used as a means of immobilizing patients. I learned quickly during my stay at Youthdale not to cry, argue, or "act out" in any way. I was never taken away like the boy in the above vignette, so I do not know from firsthand experience what happened when patients were taken away. But witnessing fellow patients being taken away for minor offenses, hearing the yelling abruptly end, not seeing these patients for days, and witnessing their increased compliance upon return frightened me enough to act as a deterrent. My

---

[178] Fabris & Aubrecht, "Chemical constraint: Experiences of psychiatric coercion, restraint, and detention as carceratory techniques," p. 187.

reduction in apparent symptoms during my stay in the unit was not due to an increase in mental health or capacity to handle my emotions; instead, my apparent improvement was coerced through fear.

Along with the threat of complete isolation as a tool to produce compliance was the isolation that I experienced even among the other patients. One evening I was watching television with the group, staring in silence at the screen's flashing images that I had no say in or control over. A teenage girl who had recently entered the unit, but whom I assumed from her behaviour had been there before, said something under her breath. She was staring blankly at the screen so I wasn't sure if she had actually said anything. I turned my head to her. She then whispered harshly for me not to look at her and I understood. She was trying to engage in secret communication by whispering inaudibly while demonstrating the body language of simply watching TV. While her courage stirred my need for human contact, my fear prevented me from engaging with her. More than anything, I wanted out and I knew that any disobedience would increase my time there. I was immobilized. My desire for human connection and communication was overridden by my fear. I was completely isolated even as I sat in a room with other incarcerated youth.

Community is essential to healing. Community among mad and psychiatrized people can be particularly empowering. I longed to connect with the other teenage girls in the unit. I wanted to ask them about their lives and tell them about mine. Yet we shared only quick glances. We were being monitored at all times and direct communication between us was not allowed. Not all psych wards are like this. When I hear stories from other psychiatric survivors who were locked up in units where patients were free to talk to each other, my skin prickles with jealousy. On the subject of isolation and community, Irit Shimrat writes:

> Awful as it is to be locked up on a psych ward, at least we patients have each other. When I've been inside, I have always experienced a sense

of belonging. Many of us were able and willing to listen to each other's stories with the patience, gentleness, humour, and empathy lacking in our keepers. Ironically, we got a real sense of community from—and were helped to regain our ability to function by—other 'sick' people.[179]

Community is powerful. Encouraging community among mad and psychiatrized people offers opportunities for healing, growth, and empowerment. Yet psychiatry takes a risk when it allows such community to flourish. This kind of community offers mad and psychiatrized people tools to resist becoming compliant. In the lockdown unit, I was denied even the simple pleasure of conversation, contributing to my willingness to submit to their demands in order to get out as fast as possible.

Coercion and Chemical Incarceration

The days in the locked unit are mainly quiet. The opportunity to speak with staff members about what brought me here is rare. On one such occasion, in a private room with a staff member, I am told that I have a chemical imbalance in my brain. I ask how they came to this conclusion. The staff member simply repeats that chemical imbalances are what cause behavior such as mine. I ask how she knows this. She evades answering the question, telling me that I am being difficult and uncooperative. I explain that I am concerned about unnecessarily being medicated. I explain that I haven't yet had a chance to discuss the reasons I am so unhappy. I explain that I worry about medication being overprescribed. She tells me I am being paranoid. She tells me that successful completion of this program, and prompt release, is dependent on my cooperation.

Liat Ben-Moshe points out that psychiatrized people are framed as "not competent enough to refuse treatment"

---

[179] Shimrat, "The tragic farce of 'community mental healthcare,'" p. 154.

yet "ironically... people's competency is rarely questioned when giving consent to treatment."[180] Psychiatric medications were presented to me as positive, helpful, and necessary. My questions and critiques were dismissed, and framed as symptomatic of my mental illness through the use of words like "uncooperative" and "paranoid." At the same time, my apparent inability to make rational decisions was never framed as an impediment to my ability to consent to medication, only as an impediment to my ability to refuse it.

These coercive tactics are examples of gaslighting, and they worked to secure my compliance. Psychiatry uses gaslighting techniques to undermine psychiatrized people's faith in their ability to assess reality and make decisions for themselves. Kris Nelson describes gaslighting as "a tactic used to destabilize your understanding of reality, making you constantly doubt your own experiences."[181] Gaslighting is frequently used by abusers to make their victims doubt that there is anything abusive happening. Gaslighting shifts attention away from the problematic behaviour of the abuser and onto the victim's ability to perceive, understand and make rational decisions about what is happening. While much of the writing on gaslighting as a tactic of abuse focuses on its use within abusive intimate relationships, gaslighting also takes place within psychiatry.

When my completely valid and rational suggestion that more time should be spent considering the reasons for my unhappiness (given the circumstance of sexual abuse) was dismissed as me being difficult and uncooperative, that is an example of gaslighting. When my legitimate concern about the over-prescription of medication was dismissed as paranoia, that is another example of gaslighting. If the goal was to promote healing and wellness, questions and considerations about my own treatment would be welcomed. The use of gaslighting reveals that the goal of psychiatry/

---

180 Ben-Moshe, "Alternatives to (disability) incarceration," p. 262.

181 Nelson, "Gaslighting is a common victim-blaming abuse tactic – Here are 4 ways to recognize it in your life." para. 17.

psychiatrized environments is not healing and wellness, but compliance.

These coercive practices were an attempt to implement what Fabris and Aubrecht refer to as chemical incarceration. They define chemical incarceration as "mandatory drugging.[182] of people considered mad or mentally ill but also anyone in an institution who is drugged without informed consent, with or without diagnosis."[183] The dismissal of my concerns and the use of gaslighting and coercion do not amount to informed consent. Eventually, I agreed to begin taking psychiatric medication despite not wanting to and not believing it would help me. I did so in order to appear cooperative and compliant in the hope that it would result in early release. Not only was I physically incarcerated in that I was kept in an enclosed space and not allowed to leave, my body was further incarcerated by the introduction of unwanted chemicals intended to change my behaviour.

I experienced this medication as a dulling of my senses and a diminishing of initiative and desire. The drugs felt to me like low-grade dissociation but in an ongoing way without any respite or release. It was as if the world became muted. The urgency that I had felt before which drove me to self-injury, overdose and other forms of traumatic "acting out" was gone. That urgency, however, was an embodied resistance to my oppressive circumstances. Without it, the unbearable became acceptable. Fabris and Aubrecht write, "[the] term chemical incarceration makes it possible to consider psychiatric drugging as a form of legitimized violence intended to restrain movement, remove agency, and deny self-determination."[184] This was my experience. Psychiatry worked not only to produce a compliant patient, but also a compliant daughter who would no longer call attention to abuse.

---

[182] Fabris & Aubrecht, "Chemical constraint: Experiences of psychiatric coercion, restraint, and detention as carceratory techniques."

[183] Fabris & Aubrecht, "Chemical constraint: Experiences of psychiatric coercion, restraint, and detention as carceratory techniques," p. 187.

[184] Fabris & Aubrecht, "Chemical constraint: Experiences of psychiatric coercion, restraint, and detention as Carceratory Techniques," p. 190.

Double Violation

At night, the day staff leave and the night staff arrive. At night, my glasses are taken from me and I lie on a rubber mattress with a too-thin blanket covering me in an empty room with a covered window. The night staff sit in the hallway while the patients sleep. Tonight, I am in incredible pain. I get migraines, brought on by stress, and tonight I am experiencing an awful one. I toss and turn and try to ignore the pain but it is unbearable. In tears, I leave the room and approach the night staff, a woman I do not know. I tell her that I am in so much pain and can't sleep. She takes me into the main space where my days are spent, which is frightening and ominous in the dark. The night doctor, an older man I do not know, looks over my chart as I sit before him desperate and helpless. He tells me that I have a history of overdosing and therefore he cannot offer me any pain medication. I plead with him for just one Tylenol. He closes my chart, telling me no. Instead he offers to massage my neck to relieve the tension. He retrieves a bottle from the shelf and squirts a lotion into his hands. To my horror, he begins to touch me, rubbing my shoulders and neck. I sit there in the dark while he does this, not wanting his hands on me, just wanting relief from the pain. After he is finished, the night staff leads me back to my room and I lie on the mattress, sick and in pain.

This memory is perhaps the most difficult to revisit. Being a multiply disabled person who is both traumatized/ psychiatrized and also experiences chronic pain, this vignette reveals the way that being labelled "mentally ill" can be a means of denying a person the right to access healthcare that they need. While my concerns about psychiatric medication were dismissed and my history of overdose was not considered reason to avoid prescribing me pills, my need for a single, supervised Tylenol in the midst of severe pain was denied. One Tylenol would not have resulted in an overdose, but the opportunity to "teach me a lesson" about my bad behaviour was more important than administering appropriate healthcare. Not only that, but in a state of pain-induced helplessness, in a dark room with strangers, I was subjected to physical touch that was nonconsensual and extremely unwanted. As a survivor of sexual abuse, this invasive touch from an older man in the context of the helplessness of both physical pain and incarceration was traumatic.

Syrus Ware, Joan Ruzsa, and Giselle Dias describe prison as "an oppressive, violent, dehumanizing environment that worsens existing disabilities and creates new ones."[185] While the authors are writing about incarceration within prisons, psychiatric institutions can also be described as oppressive, violent, and dehumanizing. Psychiatric institutions similarly worsen existing disabilities and create new ones. The disabling effects of trauma are compounded by the violent and abusive treatment within psychiatric institutions. Rather than addressing the initial violence that produced the trauma and resulted in the traumatic "acting out," psychiatry uses violence, coercion, and fear in order to produce compliance. While the short-term effect of this was that I took the medication they prescribed and stopped "acting out" for the time being, this apparent "recovery" was not sustainable. The original trauma had not been addressed; instead, it had been added to by experiences like the one described above. Upon release into the community, I was not "cured." I was more traumatized than ever. Despite attempts to further my incarceration by keeping me medicated, I stopped taking the pills. My traumatic "acting out" continued and escalated. However, I no longer believed that anyone could help me.

Even more than the traumatic experience of having to shower and stand naked in front of a stranger upon entering the psychiatric facility, this experience of being massaged in the dark by an older man deeply affected me. The helplessness of being in extreme pain, the fact that this man was older and therefore reminded me of my grandfather who sexually abused me, the fact that I was uncomfortable with any kind of physical touch, the darkness of the room, all of this combined to make this experience particularly traumatic. I told no one

---

[185] Ware, Ruzsa & Dias, "It can't be fixed because it's not broken: Racism and disability in the Prison Industrial Complex," p. 174.

about it for years. It found a place in the half-thought thoughts that store the traumatic memories I find too unbearable to think of. This experience sums up what Cresswell describes as the "double violation" of psychiatry:

> Self-harm survivor knowledge, to sum up, may be viewed as structured in terms of a perceived *double violation*. In violation #1, the survivor is survivor of the gendered trauma of childhood; in violation #2 the survivor is survivor of those medical models which are conventionally presented as treatments.[186]

The hands of the doctor on my neck and shoulders echoed my grandfather's hands. I was violated again.

Un/Marked Bodies

I left the unit medicated despite the fact that I did not want to be medicated. I learned that the quickest way to get out was to comply. I got out and shortly thereafter came off the meds and dropped out of high school. Years passed. I am now seventeen and extremely drunk. I am at a party and I don't know the difference between coolers and hard liquor. I grab a twenty sixer of some kind of liquor out of the hands of some teenager. I tip it back and drink. I hear the words "CHUG CHUG CHUG" and then blackness. My hand is up in the air holding a piece of glass, my arm is bleeding. My parents are holding me down against my will. I am struggling, screaming, biting. The police officer is riding with me in the ambulance. I wake up the next day remembering only pieces from the night before, still too drunk to understand the weight of them. I am in the psych ward, in an empty room, on a bed. A nurse comes in with a small paper cup and hands it to me. Inside is a pill. She tells me to take my medication. I tell her I am not on any medication. She becomes visibly irritated and tells me just to take it. I tell her again, emboldened by my drunkenness, that I am not on any medication. I demand to know what she is trying to give me. She tells me it is a starting dose of Effexor (an antidepressant).

---

[186] Cresswell, "Psychiatric "survivors" and testimonies of self-harm," p. 1675, emphasis in original.

Despite my best efforts to avoid psychiatry, I found myself locked up within two years of my release from Youthdale. This time I was only kept in the psych ward for a few days. During that time, I was kept alone in a room with just a bed in it. When I initially arrived, and was still very drunk, I was screaming that I didn't belong there. I was also screaming about being sexually abused. As I sobered up I realized that I needed to act compliant, because I did not want to risk being incarcerated for an extended period of time. I attempted to pass off my behaviour as an unfortunate incident of drinking too much. Both my behaviour and my psychiatric history indicated otherwise.

Again, my naming of the sexual violence that I had experienced was not addressed. Again, the problem was located in my body. Again, psychiatric medication was pushed upon me without regard for my consent. The nurse who attempted to coerce me into taking a starting dose of Effexor was the first person to speak to me the morning after my arrival. A drunk person who has not yet had a sober conversation with a doctor cannot give informed consent to starting a new medication. I don't even think it is safe for a drunk person to take most psychiatric medication. However, the imperative to have me medicated was as strong in this psych ward as it was in Youthdale.

Medicating me would be a way to extend the space of the psych ward beyond its walls. It would be another way, beyond fear of incarceration, to continue the compliance which incarceration attempts to produce. Fabris and Aubrecht point out that "contrary to the notion of safe and effective treatment, drugging is not 'less restrictive' than a cage because our very thoughts and feelings are compromised, restraining people physically, and diverting our will to escape."[187] Despite their attempts at coercion I managed to leave the ward un-medicated. I was as cooperative as possible, assuring the doctors that it had been a bad night of drinking that wouldn't happen again.

---

[187] Fabris and Aubrecht, "Chemical constraint: Experiences of psychiatric coercion, restraint, and detention as carceratory techniques," p. 196.

This vignette also highlights that when psychiatrized people are understood as dangerous, the police may be involved. This was the first time, but not the last, that my behaviour was framed as a threat not only to myself but to other people. A police escort accompanied me to the hospital indicating that I was understood as dangerous. My race and class contributed to my being brought to a psych ward rather than a police station, and to my not experiencing police violence or being charged. Appeals against psychiatric incarceration often highlight psychiatrized people who are not framed as violent, citing that it is unnecessary to lock up people who aren't dangerous. For example, Fabris and Aubrecht write "I was hauled into an emergency ward for acting 'strange' at work, which like most such experiences was not dangerous.[188]

While it is important to acknowledge that many psychiatrized people are incarcerated for nonviolent behaviour, it is also important to consider whose violence results in incarceration and whose does not. The police officer who rode in the ambulance with me did not follow up on any of the accusations of sexual abuse that I was drunkenly yelling about. I have been incarcerated multiple times for my behaviour. The white men in my family who were responsible for my abuse have not. I do not advocate for incarceration in any case as I find incarceration to be inherently violent, but I think it is important to consider who experiences incarceration and who does not. It is also important to consider what kinds of incarceration various people experience. I was marked as mentally ill but not criminal. My abusers were not marked by the violence they enacted.

The Extended Psych Ward/Failure to Comply

Many years have passed. Despite avoiding psychiatry to the best of my ability, I have been formed and detained a number of times. I have

---

188 Fabris and Aubrecht, "Chemical constraint: Experiences of psychiatric coercion, restraint, and detention as carceratory techniques," p. 189.

escaped from a hospital after waking up there, knowing that they would form me as soon as they discovered who I was. Despite being in so much pain, I do not trust psychiatry to help me. My teenage years and early twenties included multiple suicide attempts, persistent self-injury, perpetual re-traumatization, and years of active alcoholism. I am now twenty-six. I have found non-psychiatric counselling and non-psychiatric addiction support. I am seven months sober and more stable than I have been for many years. I have not had a family doctor since childhood and I am at an intake appointment for a new family doctor. The doctor asks me questions about my family's medical history. She asks me questions about my medical history. I am honest with her about my past but explain the supports I have in place and that I am sober and stable. She stops typing on her computer and turns to face me. She tells me that with my history of concurrent disorders I will need to be medicated. She tells me she will refer me to CAMH (the Centre for Addiction and Mental Health) where I can receive treatment for both my addiction issues and mood disorders. I tell her that won't be necessary. I explain that I am doing well and accessing support that is working for me. I just need a family doctor for things like cancer screenings and basic healthcare. She tells me I am only seven months sober and that there is no way I will remain sober if I don't get the proper treatment. I tell her I don't want to go to CAMH or be medicated, that the supports I have are working and I am confident that I will be able to remain sober. She gets up abruptly and starts to leave the room. I ask her where she is going. She tells me that she will not be my doctor because I am refusing to accept the help that I need.

This final vignette drives home the fact that the goal of psychiatry is not healing or wellness but compliance. When I arrived at the intake appointment with this doctor, I was expecting routine questions about my health. I did not expect that my psychiatric history would be used to deny me access to healthcare unless I consented to being medicated and re-psychiatrized, something that I definitely did not want. The doctor told me that I would not be able to maintain my sobriety. At the time of writing this article, I am 3.5 years sober (at the time of editing this book for publication I am 9 years sober) and I have remained sober without going to CAMH and without being medicated.

This vignette illustrates that the space of psychiatry extends beyond the enclosures of psych wards and institutions for psychiatrized people. Psychiatry continues the work of producing compliance. It does so through coerced and forced medication, gaslighting, refusal to provide services such as healthcare, and threat of further harm or re-incarceration. Psychiatric survivors continue to be coerced and controlled even after we have left the physical spaces of incarceration. We are not trusted to make decisions about our health. We are not permitted to define our own reality. Psychiatric survivor testimonies such as this reclaim reality from the authority of psychiatry. By writing our stories, we refuse to comply.

Conclusion

The traumatic "acting out" of my teenage years and the first half of my 20s represented an embodied resistance to trauma. Self-injury, suicide attempts, alcoholism, and overdosing worked both to manage my overwhelming feelings and to make clear that something was very wrong. My childhood attempts to stop or escape abuse proved futile. My traumatic "acting out" worked as an alternate means of resistance and an embodied testimony to the reality of what I was experiencing. My self-injury resulted in my never having to see my sexually abusive grandfather again. My drunken behaviour, while resulting in regular re-traumatization, also functioned as an obvious sign that there was something very wrong that needed addressing. My suicide attempts were clear messages that my life was unbearably painful and that I needed help.

Instead of help, however, I received more violence. Psychiatry has, multiple times and through multiple means, attempted to silence the call of my traumatic "acting out." Instead of helping me to get free from violence and to heal from its effects, psychiatry encouraged my continued silence. The goal was to produce a person too terrified, too exhausted, or too drugged to resist. I offer this essay as testimony to what I have lived, hoping that it will be "witnessed as an event about which 'something ought to be done.'"[189]

I join with the psychiatric survivors, mad pride activists, writers, and zinesters who come before me, offering my story as one of many who have survived psychiatry. I offer myself as a witness for those who have stories yet to tell. I am a traumatized person who lives with the impacts of repetitive and sustained violences, but I have found ways to honour my truth and protect myself. Psychiatry, despite its best efforts, has failed to make me comply.

---

[189] Cresswell, "Psychiatric "survivors" and testimonies of self-harm," p. 1672.

Being Good
Will Never
Solve the
Problem
Because the
Problem is Not
That
I am Bad

The house isn't safe. The incest, subtle, implied, threatened and actual, is not safe. The sexual abuse that I grew up with that turned my body into terror, is not safe. The wilderness is safe, the trees upon trees, the endless forest, the animals that move through darkness. The night is safe.

Popular representations of witchcraft, possessions, and exorcisms are tied up with scripts of incest and sexual abuse. Feminine bodies are positioned as inherently sexual, dangerous and out of control. Literal conduits of evil. Have you ever wondered why the majority of exorcism movies are about young, teenage girls who are at the age of puberty? These are scripts about feminine sexuality as inherently disordered, as inherently 'asking for it'. These are male fantasies, locating sexual violence in the victim's bodies, locating the source of violence in the 'devil', the 'witch'.

Stories about 'evil witches' which present feminine sexualities, feminine bodies, feminine aging, nature, wilderness and animals as the source and cause of evil, as the threat to the safety of the home, the family, turn reality on its head. I have wandered naked in the wilderness, under the moonlight, and I was absolutely safe there. Where it wasn't safe to be naked, where it wasn't safe at all, was the home. My home, my family: these were the sources of violence. Not my body, not my sexuality, not the forest, not the night.

Calling myself a witch is about more than naming my spirituality, my affinity with more-than-human worlds, my connection with the living universe – it is a political act, a political naming. Calling myself a witch is aligning myself with the forest, with the feminine, with my body, with the night. Calling myself a witch is declaring that I do not believe the misogynist propaganda about witches that has been used to justify violence for hundreds of years. Calling myself a witch is an act of resistance against sexual abuse and incest. It is survival.

I lay in my bed, next to my partner, triggered beyond belief, pain ripping through my body. I feel utterly alone in the universe. My voice, the detached voice of dissociation, is caught up in compulsive telling. I am trying to tell my partner what it feels like to be an incest survivor, what it feels like to have lived a lifetime of sexual violence. The pain is crushing, overwhelming, the work of telling, futile, because I know it cannot be told.

I am staring out my bedroom window at the night sky and I see a quick flash of blackness. This movement stirs me and I look with curiosity, not knowing what I've seen. It happens again, and again, and I realize I am seeing a bat. When I recognize this bat, all the tension in my body suddenly melts away. I have never seen a bat out my bedroom window before, and tonight, as I struggle to tell the story of incest, to bear witness to the obliterating pain in my body, the bat appears. I know, as a witch, that this bat appeared for me. This bat came to me, as foxes and raccoons and loons have done, to show me that I am not alone. I am here, I am seen, I am known.

As a child I would leave the house of incest and go into the night and wrap my arms around the trunk of a tree. Nonhuman beings and I have always had a spiritual understanding, a strong solidarity. I know that I cannot protect the bat and the bat cannot protect me, but we see each other, we know each other, we are in this together. The bat is a being, a part of this connected, living universe, and the bat has come to me to show me that I am too. No matter what, regardless of the sickening violence, the violations, the narratives which cover over the truth, the fact that no one can see, the bat knows, and I know, and we are in this together.

With the bat, comes calm. Far from being evil, the bat, like my body, is good. I suddenly realize how deeply I have internalized the message that I am inherently bad, inherently disordered, inherently wrong. I suddenly see how I have lost touch with night, how I have ingested the lie which turns reality on its head. I have located the violence within me. I have worked hard and long to redeem myself, to exorcise myself, to become 'good'. Suddenly the words form in my mind: Being good will never solve the problem because the problem is not that I am bad. The problem in not the bat, the witch, the wilderness, the night, the forest, the feminine, my body, my being. The problem is incest, sexual violence, and a culture that sustains these things.

Being a witch is my safety, my power, my refusal. Witchcraft is my communion with so many other beings, it is my relationship, my solidarity, my connection with a universe that loves me. The wilderness is safe, the trees upon trees, the endless forest, the animals that move through darkness. The night is safe.

Intoxication Spaces

(Part Two)

My sobriety does not mean, however, that I have come into alignment with the dominant maps of intoxication culture. As it gets later in the evening, Queen Street West ceases to be a space of shopping and transforms into a space of drinking. The bars which line the streets become the only sanctioned spaces to socialize. Social drinking, meaning controlled drinking under socially sanctioned circumstances, becomes the expected and demanded activity. As a sober alcoholic, the space becomes a mental map of exclusion. I cannot partake in the activities which the space is designed for. The coffee shops close early and if you aren't drinking or comfortable being around large amounts of drinking, there are few places to go.

My mental map of sobriety is entirely different from my alcoholic mental map. It includes: bars I don't feel at home in, finding the few coffee shops which are open later, an awareness of the 12 step meetings happening in the area, and a recognition of other people in 12 step recovery programs who I see on the street, share knowing looks with, and pass in respect for anonymity. Again, my mental map of sobriety is different from the mental maps of other sober people due to a number of factors including the reasons for our sobriety, whether or not we attend 12 step meetings, practice another form of recovery, or remain sober in other ways, and how comfortable we feel around drinking. My mental map of sobriety, while strikingly different from my alcoholic mental map, is simultaneously quite similar. Both maps are superimposed on the dominant map of intoxication culture. Both maps require navigating and negotiating with a dominant map that does not include me.

Space is not simply 'there', organically evolving into what it happens to be. Space is conceived of and produced in particular ways in service of capitalism, colonialism, and other systems of power. As Razack explains, space is conceived with intended purpose, perceived through daily experience and lived as a negotiation with and interpretation of conceived and perceived uses of space.[190] As Ingram, Bouthillette and

---

[190] Razack, "When place becomes race."

Retter point out, mental maps map subjective experience of space based on social location and lived experience.[191] These mental maps can affirm, resist, undermine or re-inscribe the dominant maps.

Intoxication culture has its own dominant maps. Non-normative substance users who are excluded or punished by intoxication culture have mental maps which do not align with the dominant maps of intoxication spaces. I have reflected on my own experience as a non-normative substance user, first as an active alcoholic, then as a sober alcoholic. My experiences reveal two very different mental maps, neither of which aligns with the dominant map of intoxication culture. These maps are only two examples of the vast number of mental maps which are produced through normative and non-normative relationships to substances. Thinking through substance use in terms of mental mapping reveals that our relationships to substances shape our relationships to space.

---

[191] Ingram et al, "Narratives of place: Subjective and collective."

Can Theory
Be A Spell?
(Part Two)

I am doing my readings but I am not writing anything.
I am writing in my journal every morning.
I am not writing anything scholarly.
I happen to see a book: *Caliban and the Witch: Women, the Body and Primitive Accumulation* by Silvia Federici.
I buy this book. I start reading it.
My partner asks me shouldn't I be reading my course work? I tell them, *I know, I know.*

I got to a get together with one of the professors I am working with, and two other grad students, also working with this professor.
We talk about what is going on in our work.
I talk about how stuck I am, how hard I am finding it to bring poetry into conversation with theory.
I wonder out loud why it is so difficult.
One thing comes to mind. In scholarship I must cite all my sources.
I must meticulously track the production of knowledge.
I can't say what I learned from the bottom of the river.[192]
It won't be taken seriously. I will need a source to back that up.
But in poetry, I can.
I can say what I learned from the river.
I can say: the river. It doesn't need to be correct.
Poetry can't be wrong because it is
not trying to be right.

Magic is pulsing in my blood as I say these words.
Witchcraft is unarticulated and on the tip of my tongue.

We talk about this. One topic unfolds into another.
The other two grad students are comic artists
and they are showing their work.
We are talking about creative process.

---

[192] The Don River.

Another thing comes to mind.
In scholarship I am making an argument.
I am trying to prove a thesis.
I am trying to make a point.
In poetry I am not trying to prove anything.
I am simply showing.
I am opening my experience to page.
In scholarship I aim for control, precision, accuracy.
In poetry I surrender. I am a conduit. A channel.
The professor tells me that scholarship does not
need to be this way.
Yes, this kind of writing is privileged with the academy,
but it is not the only kind of theory.
There are other kinds of theory.
We are invited to consider what theory might be.

The conversation continues.
One of the students mentions that washing dishes
is often a time when ideas which have been stuck
come flowing free.
We all agree on that.
Later in the conversation something is said
which reminds me of *Caliban and the Witch.*
I pull it out of my bag, wrinkled
from when I accidentally poured water all over it,
and explain that I've been reading it,
even though it isn't related to what I'm
supposed to be reading for my course.
I just saw it and had to read it.
The professor and the grad students
exclaim that it is related.
Of course it is.
I laugh. I admit that I'm a witch.
I wonder

Can theory be a spell?

I go home with a full head and an open heart.

I linger in the thoughts and the impressions.
I make my lunch, say my blessings, eat.
I begin to wash the dishes, warm soapy water, slippery
glass and metal.
Suddenly, a flood, almost incomprehensible but
I turn off the tap, quickly dry my hands on the
dishtowel, grab my journal where it was sitting on
the table and begin to make notes.

Can theory be a spell?

At the basis magic was an animistic conception of
nature that did not admit to any separation between
matter and spirit, and thus imagined the cosmos as a
living organism, populated by occult forces, where every
element was in "sympathetic" relation with the rest.[193]

– Silvia Federici

This conception of nature, this lack of separation
between matter and spirit, this understanding of the cosmos
as a living organism, is something I have always known. Deep
down in my very being, in my very cells, I have always known.
The words for it, I did not always have. As Federici explains
in great detail, this conception of the cosmos was violently
punished and silenced, through the medieval European witch
hunts, and through colonial conquest. The truth of this magic,
in all the varied ways it was known and understood, was all
but erased. Yet it lives on. Spiritual traditions and cosmologies
which understand this connectedness continue to exist today.
Indigenous cultures continue to uphold cosmologies and
traditions which honour this aliveness. And the remains of
what was called witchcraft in Europe, and in places where
Europeans colonized, continues to survive, sometimes only
in fragments, but those fragments are lovingly restored to
life.

---

[193] Federici, *Caliban and the witch*, p. 141-142.

My ancestors lived in Ireland, Scotland, and England. My Scottish and English ancestors experienced the witch hunts Federici describes. My Irish ancestors also experienced a violent disconnection from their beliefs, though this was orchestrated largely through English colonization. Part of my practice as a witch is reaching back in time and finding the fragments.

There is a huge sense of loss, an emptiness,
rooted in capitalism and colonialism.
There is a disconnection from the stories, the
practices, the magic which used to animate the world.
As a child, I found this magic intuitively,
without knowing that it was, at its core,
the same magic my ancestors knew.
I found this magic in relationship,
relationship with plants, animals, landscapes, and
weather.
I found this magic far away from the land of my
ancestors,
on colonized land which has been violently disconnected
from the people who have been in relationship with it
for countless generations.
Though I did not have the words for this as a child,
resistance to colonialism is an important part
of my understanding of witchcraft and magic,
especially in the context of being in relationship with
this place, this land.

Nothing in my child-world made sense.
My parents taught me about justice
and then did me the greatest injustice
by offering me up to my grandfather,
who sexually abused me, my sister, my cousins.
I had no bodily autonomy, no safety,
and my world made no sense.
Amidst this terror and abandonment
I was sustained by magic.

I didn't know the word 'magic' then.
I didn't know what my ancestors had always known,
and yet, somehow, I did.
I knew, in my very being, that the universe was alive.
Pine, maple, birch, the forest,
the sky, the lake, the loons, the chickadees,
these were my first, and most sustaining relationships.
The wonder that I felt at sunrise and sunset,
the endless stars stretching out far past this planet.
I was in a world alive.

A world so much bigger than the tiny cottage
with curtains instead of doors
where so much shame and terror and violence
took place every day.
That cottage wasn't everything.
That cottage wasn't the truth.
There was a greater truth
and that truth is how I survived,
and how I continue to live today.

Federici writes "Above all, magic seemed a form of refusal of work, of insubordination, and an instrument of grassroots resistance to power. The world had to be "disenchanted" in order to be dominated."[194] As a child-witch who used magic to survive, these words resonate deeply. Magic is resistance. Magic is refusal. Magic works from the ground up. It is expansive. It is ubiquitous. It is a source of strength for those who use it.

Despite the forced powerlessness which capitalism and colonialism work to impose, magic resists. This is why it was a threat deemed dangerous enough to warrant a thorough and violent attack. Despite the forced powerlessness of being a child living in a house of incest and sexual violence, magic sustained me. In my case my rituals were branded as madness, landing me in a psych ward. In my opinion, this incarceration

---

[194] Federici, *Caliban and the witch*, p. 174.

and violence continues the work of the witch hunts, under different names.

What is the difference between a crazy person and a witch? Both experience the world in ways which defy an 'objective', capitalist, colonial worldview.

Can theory be a spell?

Lockup instilled a new kind of fear in me. The deadening which was imposed on me took its toll. Defending my magic became harder and harder. Remembering the aliveness of the world became harder and harder. I shrunk into a new kind of madness, not one of connection, but one of severe disconnection. I was alone. Completely alone in the universe. This is what my magic had saved me from. You can never be alone in a living universe. But psychiatrization, lack of community where I might have met other crazy witches, and ongoing sexual violence took its toll. I lost my way and I lost my magic. The universe solidified into dead matter, something which I had been taught to believe it was all along. Suicide loomed. Pills bottles and bathtubs. I couldn't live in a dead world all alone.

Then I found alcohol, oblivion to drown out oblivion. I fell into the allure of alcoholism, which is, as I understand it, an inverted quest for magic. Instead of a living universe, a dead one, but the bottle offered momentary release. Drunk out of my mind, possibility seemed to open up again, like it used to when I knew the universe was alive. But the bottle made the universe contract even further, turning everything into nothing, including myself. I needed the bottle to connect at all, and because of the bottle, I was completely unable to connect. Such is the paradox of addiction, as sickness, which as I understand it, results from trauma and manifests as a longing for and inability to find: spirit, meaning, connection, relationship, *magic*.

I lost nine years, my self-respect, my values, my truths. I came up for air on the other side when an acquaintance asked "why don't you try 12 steps?" and because I could see the magic in her, I listened. I went to my first meeting and found a community of people in various stages of recovery. People who described with complete accuracy the soul sickness I was in the throes of. People who, without using the word, talked about magic. People who were in the process of reenchanting the universe and in doing so, saving their lives. For the first time in many years I felt the sparkle, the stirring deep down, the urging, the remembering. I was just beginning to wake up.

Can theory be a spell?

> In thinking about our day we may face indecision. We may not be able to determine which course to take. Here we ask God for inspiration, an intuitive thought or a decision. We relax and take it easy. We don't struggle. We are often surprised how the right answers come after we have tried this for a while. What used to be the hunch or the occasional inspiration gradually becomes a working part of the mind. Being still inexperienced and having just made conscious contact with God, it is not probably that we are going to be inspired at all times. We might pay for this presumption in all sorts of absurd actions and ideas. Nevertheless, we find that our thinking will, as time passes, be more and more on the plane of inspiration. We come to rely upon it.[195]
>
> – *Alcoholics Anonymous*

> We have found much of heaven and we have been rocketed into a fourth dimension of existence of which we had not even dreamed.[196]
>
> –*Alcoholics Anonymous*

Finding myself on the plane of inspiration, in the fourth dimension of existence, is to remember myself in a

[195] *Alcoholics Anonymous.*

[196] *Alcoholics Anonymous.*

world of magic, a world that is, in Federici's words, *"a living organism."*[197] I light my candles on my altar. I go outside, barefoot, water the plants and watch for the bees. I pay attention to the moon getting fat, then slivering down, disappearing. I notice coincidences, or, what Carl Jung called "synchronicity."[198] I recognize that the universe is alive, that I am a part of that life, and that I can tap into this magic to guide me. I can choose to seek this magic, to align myself with this magic. I can choose to pay attention.

Every day is practice of paying attention, of remembering, of entering into a sustaining relationship. Mysobriety and my very life depend on it. I no longer need the bottle because I remember magic. I turn myself toward the world, open myself to it. Every action I take is an action rooted in relationship. Every choice I make is guided by this surrender to a power greater than myself. I no longer live in a dead world all alone. My pain is held by a feeling world, a world also in pain. My power is rooted in a living world, a world filled with powers.

Can theory be a spell?

Magic saved my life. Reenchanted me.
Opened up possibility beyond the dead end of
another alley, another bottle, another hangover,
another concussion.
Magic reminded me of what I already know:
the living pulse, the aliveness of the universe.
Each day my practice, my craft, sustains me.
This work keeps me sober, keeps me healing,
keeps me growing.
This is life saving work.
Not a hobby, or an interest,
but a worldview I am remembering.
A worldview of my ancestors,

---

[197] Silvia Federici, *Caliban and the witch*, p. 141.

[198] Jung, *Synchronicity*.

a worldview I felt intuitively as a child.
A worldview that was violently taken from my
ancestors, and from the world.
A worldview that was violently taken from me.
I work to remember this magic. To save my life.
To find an answer other than bottles, pills, suicide
attempts.
To find the connection that can sustain me,
with which I can flourish.
To centre myself in community. To seek justice.

I search for fragments of the magic of my own ancestors, knowing that they will remain incomplete, but that, like seeds, they include a blueprint. This is a process I am undertaking, seeking the stories, knowledges, and traditions of Ireland, Scotland, and England. At the same time, recognizing that I exist in another time, place, and context than my ancestors did. The plants, animals, landscapes, and ecosystems which I have grown up in relationship with, are different, and therefore my magic will be different. I will create new magic in the here and now, in conversation with my ancestors, with this land, and with the communities I share space with. A commitment to magic is always a commitment to justice, to learning and unlearning, to forging relationship.

Relearning this magic means remembering my body and the world I am in relationship with. Remembering the moon and the way my body relates to it. Remembering the seasons, the cycles, the relationship between earth, rain, seed, flower, bee. Learning these relationships in an embodied way, then being moved to action in commitment to these relationships. Being moved. Movement. All around me, and inside of me, there are countless relationships. It is these relationships which are the heart of magic. Honouring these relationships, this reciprocity, is the heart of what it means to be a witch.

Can theory be a spell?

Three years sober and I applied to grad school. Unsure of how I would readjust to academia, I plunged in anyway. A witch friend of mine offered me a mason jar of lavender and a pdf of Karen Barad's "Nature's Queer Performativity."

"You'll like this" she said.

Reading Barad I felt the prickle of recognition on my skin. I felt the tears in my eyes and the pull on my heart. I saw magic. I felt myself light up with possibility. Using the language of physics this scholar was reenchanting the universe.

Barad's theory worked on me. The way poetry does. The way 12 steps do. The way magic does. Barad's theory had me reorienting, remembering, turning toward the beings all around me, and inside me, noticing.

Barad paints a picture of a universe alive, a universe which does not privilege the human, or even the animal, or even the animate, as the only actor. Barad proposes "an agential realist ontology, or what one might call a 'quantum ontology', based on the existence of phenomena rather than of independently existing things."[199] Barad writes "entanglements are not intertwinings of separate entities but rather irreducible relationships of responsibility. There is no fixed dividing line between 'self' and 'other', 'past' and 'present' and 'future', 'here' and 'now', 'cause' and 'effect.'"[200] Barad reveals a world of entanglement, a world in which we are never radically separate, but instead are always in relationship, are in fact the very stuff of relationship. Barad reminds us of the responsibility that is inherent in this worldview.

It sounds to me like magic.

Can theory be a spell?

Despite Barad's quantum physics, I go to school and I don't mention magic much. In a performance class I create a

---

[199] Barad, "Nature's queer performativity," p. 45.

[200] Barad, "Nature's queer performativity," p. 46.

performance exploring my experience of psychiatrization and of being a witch. In most classes I do not go this far. I try to find other ways to talk about the same things. I say the 'nonhuman' instead of the 'living universe' (which includes the human, as well as the animate and inanimate nonhumans, and even other nonhumans whose very existence I feel I can't mention, like the fairies of the Other World who were central to my Irish ancestors cosmology, like the energies I sense and know, but can't name). I stick to 'nonhuman' and take animal studies and talk about plants and get excited about the collapse of the wave function and read about environmental justice. I say everything I need to say except for what's at the heart of it. Because I don't know how to say what's at the heart of it. I am here, in the university, under the weight of cold 'objectivity', a complete dismissal and disdain of spirit, and a lack of serious inquiry into what is meant by the word 'witch'.

In my spare time, which is limited as a grad student, I work with my sponsors in 12 step programs, I practice my craft, I read books about the beliefs of my ancestors, I learn about plants, I seek deeper connection, deeper awareness, deeper remembrance of magic. I procrastinate on my 'real work', my assignments and class readings, to do this 'other' work, this personal work, this life saving work, this utterly central work, of magic. The gap between my academic work and my magic widens. The tension increases. I feel like a liar. I feel dishonest. I feel cut apart. I feel unable to say what I mean, always seeking ways to say it without really saying it. I carve apart my life and my different ways of knowing, setting what I think will be seen as valid and acceptable on one side, leaving the rest in the garden, at the altar.

I don't want to write theory anymore. I don't want to be in the university. I don't want to keep telling half-truths. I feel deadened by this work the way I felt deadened by the psychward. Which is a very dangerous thing for me, as an alcoholic whose sobriety and survival depends on my remembering of magic.

So, I surrender. I write this rambling paper. I dive down into magic and I try to bring it closer to theory. I dare to say the things in a paper that I have been afraid to say. I dare to name magic as an organizing principle in all of my work, as a central analytic functioning unnamed in the background. I write these words as an offering, as an attempt to get honest, as a practice of both theory and magic. I have to ask

Can theory be a spell?

Fucking Crazy:

On Complex Trauma,

Surviving Sexual Violence,

and Living My Best Slut Life

I am too sick to write this paper. I am nauseous. I have a headache. My muscles are tense. My skin is on fire. I have been crying uncontrollably followed by numb hours blanked out and scrolling my phone. My body is flooded with sensations, deep visceral apparitions of pain, which I refuse and struggle against.

I am too sick to write about sex. I don't want to write about sex because I've been thinking about incest. I've been deep in therapy work and struggling hard with my complex ptsd. I have been triggered. Memories from my childhood keep flooding back to me. I don't want to write about sex because I feel fucked up and sick and sad.

Right now in this moment I feel disinterested in sex, maybe even repulsed by it. I also feel stressed and insecure about the psoriasis that is flaring all over my body. I was reading *The Body Keeps the Score* and in it there is a study in which incest survivors were found to have higher rates of autoimmune conditions.[201] Psoriasis is autoimmune. It is hypervigilance at a cellular level. My immune system is launching an attack against a threat which isn't present, inadvertently attacking my own body. Familiar story. Trauma body. Trauma brain. Red and flaky and scaly and stressful. It is hard to feel desirable like this; it is hard to feel desire.

But then I think of the other night, having sex with my date for the first time (even though we've been lowkey long distance seeing each other for a year), and how nervous I felt about the red dots and patches all over my skin. *Your psoriasis* she gasped *It's beautiful.* And she is beautiful and good and sincere. I think about the way I let myself relax into safety, the way I let myself feel her desire and my own. I think about the way she pressed her body into mine, eager and without hesitation, the way our desire built between us and my skin was neither a detraction nor an imposition.

I think about my partner holding my psoriasis covered foot in their hand and the way they held my skin in their focus and gently brought my foot to their lips, kissing my red

[201] Vander Kolk, *The body keeps the score.*

inflamed skin. I think about the way I covered my eyes because the sight was too much to bear and then opened them again, squirming both from the pleasure and the vulnerability and the miraculous surprise of love.

As someone living with complex ptsd, who has known violence and betrayal in most of my important intimate relationships, I am not familiar with love. The combination of sexuality and care, of desire and attentiveness, is almost more than my trauma brain can process. But I do. Little by little I time travel to the present, I breathe into this body, into this hard earned safety, and I begin to trust in my pleasure, in my desire, in the transformative possibilities of all sorts of intimacies.

Thinking of this pleasure, this intimacy, this safety, helps me to time travel back to the present, now, helps me to breathe into my adult body and retrieve myself from the apparitions of terror and helplessness. Thinking about my date and my partner, people I trust and care for, gives my bodymind something else to experience other than fear and pain. Now I am thinking about pleasure and desire, intimacy and care, I am easing into the safety of the beautiful life I have today, the relationships which nurture and sustain me. Now, from this place, I want to write about sex.

She ties my wrists with her belt and leans me over the bench. She instructs her service submissive to hold my hair and my wrists. She shows me the hand signals.

This is green, this is yellow, this is orange, this is red. You can remember that right?

I nod my head eagerly, obediently. The other two submissives are in training to become Doms, they take turns hitting me with various implements, under the instruction of the head Dom.

Try this one, hit her with that, keep it in the centre of her ass cheek.

I listen to them talk amongst themselves about the different ways they can hurt me as pain explodes through my body, sharp and brilliant. My hands are changing shapes: green, green, green, yellow.

She's at yellow! *The service sub announces.* She's at yellow, okay, go easy on her. *I feel hands all over me massaging my red skin, bruises blooming. They are hitting me again and I am crying out.*

Oh I like that sound, make her make that sound again.

I am deep in sub space, watching flashes of powerful femmes move in and out of my view, feeling the weight of my body against the bench as I yield to the pain they give me.

How does it feel? *I open my mouth but all that comes out are incoherent sounds. She laughs at this,* Come on, I thought you were a writer. Tell me how it feels.

Desperate to be good I manage to yell. It hurts, it feels like pain, burning pain!

That's all I can say and they all laugh, pleased with my answer. The scene is almost over and I am given my final instructions.

You want us to hit you some more before we stop? *I nod my head eagerly.*

You need to ask for it, as loud as you can, and the number of people who turn to look, that's how many times more we'll each hit you.

Desperate for the pain they're giving me and so deep in sub space I don't care what anyone thinks, I yell at the top of my lungs I want you to keep hitting me please!

They count off fifteen people who turn their heads. I get three more sets of fifteen blows and I count them off gratefully.

As a teenager and in the first half of my twenties I ran from pain. Reading about the common trajectory of the lives of incest survivors in *The Body Keeps the Score*, I recognize myself immediately: self-injury, suicide attempts, alcoholism, re-victimization, promiscuous sex. I did everything I could to feel something other than the sensations of terror and helplessness, thwarted rage and pervasive shame, death-like depression.

These feelings and sensations kept issuing up from the deep recesses of my traumatized bodymind, they were incoherent and urgent, present and real. I did everything I could to outrun them and very often that meant drunken sex with random men who treated me like shit. I remember reaching up to kiss whatever man was currently fucking me only to hear him say *I don't kiss sluts,* unleashing in me the torrent of feelings which I was trying so hard to outrun.

Back then the sex was like the drinking. I knew it was hurting me. I knew I didn't have control over it. I knew that I often felt humiliated and violated, that I was often in danger. I also knew that these things saved me, they were necessary. I hunted for sex like my life depended on it – in many ways it did.

After the end of an abusive relationship in which I was repeatedly told that no one else would ever love me because I'm such a disgusting fucking slut, I finally managed to find non-psychiatric therapy that didn't terrify me. I finally started to get the help that I needed to face the unrelenting flood of pain. I got sober, and I began a long process of recovery that continues today.

In sobriety, I was faced with the question of my sexuality. What could healthy sexuality look like for someone like me? Would I ever be present and non-dissociative enough to enjoy sober sex? Is monogamy a healthier option for me given my history of compulsive sexuality? After a lifetime of sexual trauma can sex ever be something else, something good, something healing? How do I envision a healing sexuality for myself that does not internalize the narratives of a dominant culture which rewards monogamous heterosexuality and relegates everything else to the margins? Is it possible to be a happy, healing, queer, sober slut, in recovery from sexual trauma?

Tell me about your desires, *my partner says to me. This is an invocation, a practice of magic, calling forth from me a torrential flood. It is still hard for me to speak my desire, even after years of therapy, even in the context of love and safety.*

I could give you a massage, you could suck my cock, I could fuck you in the ass, I could go down on you, we could lie here and make out, we could snuggle and watch tv, I could tie you up and put you in my closet. *I feel my desire moving through my body as I listen to these possibilities, possibilities my partner offers up because they know they are some of my favourites. I feel the pull and pulse of pleasure, the electric excitement and expansive relaxation of trust and safety. I love the power of knowing that my desires are good, are welcome.*

I remember the time that my partner said to me I love your desires, they are beautiful and good. Even if you have desires that I don't share, I am glad that you have them, and I want you to fulfill them. *These words are magic, they are an antidote to the terror of my sexuality being taken from me, an antidote to the demand that my sexuality always be performed for the pleasures of someone else. I listen to this list with pleasant anticipation, letting desire rise from my body to direct me toward what I want.*

I have come so far. My life traces a trajectory of transformation, an alchemy in which pain and trauma are changed into pleasure and presence, joy. I often say that it is a miracle I am alive, given what my life has been. Even more so it is a miracle that I can feel what I feel, that I live a life abundant with love and sex and desire, that I am able to turn toward my body, that the sensations which rise up from me now are not only terror and pain. And yet I can't and don't want to erase the reality of my ongoing experience of pain. I don't want to replace pain with pleasure or to proclaim that I am "all better now."

Just the other day, my therapist asked me if I am feeling suicidal. I glared at her and snapped, *No I'm not feeling suicidal.* She sensed my hostility and asked me about it. *I take that question as a threat,* I told her. She looked confused. *It's a threat of incarceration,* I told her and as a psychiatric survivor I say that from a place of intimate knowledge. Suicidal ideation remains a topic I cannot discuss for fear of my freedom being taken from me, it remains an experience pushed to the margins, shamed and taboo, punished with further violence. The extent of my ongoing pain is difficult to talk about in general, it is hard to create space in a narrative of recovery for the reality that complex ptsd is a permanent disability. I will never be someone who has not been severely traumatized. I will never have a brain like someone who grew up in an environment of safety. And while I do hope for more recovery than I have now, I also know that healing will always be work that I must do.

While discussing the move toward desiring disability within disability studies, Margaret Price writes "the larger DS [disability studies] turn toward desire seems unsure of what to do with pain. In particular, it seems unsure of what to do with what I would call *unbearable pain*—that is, the sort of pain that impels one to self-injure or to consider or attempt suicide."[202] I feel resonance with the word *unbearable*, and I am reminded how many times in the last few months I have described my pain to my therapist as unbearable, intolerable. The way my pain and its depths propel me towards behaviours that I have long since left behind: self-injury, suicide.

Price's statement that unbearable pain is "the sort of pain that impels one to self-injure or to consider or attempt suicide"[203] feels like a massive validation. Up until that statement I assumed that the type of unbearable pain Price was writing about was physical pain, not emotional pain. Despite knowing better, it is still easy for me to dismiss emotional pain as less real and less painful than physical pain. The assertation that it is "all in my head," and therefore something that I should be able to overcome by the power of will is hard to shake. Succumbing to emotional pain is often framed as a sign of weakness, because really, it can't be *that bad*. Bessel van der Kolk and many others have pointed out that the binary between physical and emotional pain is a false one, and that the pain which traumatized people endure actually manifests as visceral pain in the body. This pain is often *unbearable*, driving survivors toward drugs, alcohol, sex, self-injury, suicide, anything to lift the burden of the unbearable pain.

I am also struck my Price's recognition of the seeming incompatibility between unbearable pain and desire, how difficult it is to hold, simultaneously, the depth of unbearable

---

[202] Price, "The bodymind problem and the possibilities of pain."

[203] Price, "The bodymind problem and the possibilities of pain."

pain and how badly we want to not feel it, with a desire for the lives and bodies that we do have, the specificity of disabled embodiment, the pleasures and knowledges made possible by our intimacy with unbearable pain. How do we reconcile these? In one way, I think they are irreconcilable and that it is okay to admit that. The anguish and frustration I express to my therapist when I lament, *I can't do this anymore, I can't, I can't, it's too hard,* will not be erased no matter how many moments of healing, integration, transformation, pleasure, or joy I experience. The unbearable and the transformative continue to live side by side in my body and in my life.

It is possible to love my traumatized bodymind – this particular specific life marked by so much suffering, to move toward as much healing as is possible for me, and to grieve and rage and thrash against the limits of my capacity to endure this unbearable pain. While compulsive sexuality was an anesthetic, an attempt to repress or outrun unbearable pain, conscious sexuality is a space of healing and integration, an intentional reckoning with embodied experience. Conscious sexuality is a space in which I explore the edges and contours of pleasure and pain, the way these can bleed into each other, in which I express my frustration and my desire, my numbness and my wetness, my commitment to healing and my grief at what has been taken from me. Conscious sexuality is a space in which there is intentional communication about this process, in which there is language and time for processing and unpacking, in which my body and its visceral experiences are given centre stage. I have spent years trying to suppress the messages issuing from my traumatized bodymind. Now through various practices including therapy, mindfulness, witchcraft, magic, embodied writing, and conscious sexuality, I invite my body back. I give open space for the sensations, both of pleasure and of pain, and I find language to communicate my desires, my boundaries, and my needs. This is trauma magic, a process of reclaiming what was taken from me.

Why don't you go down on Clementine? *my partner says to our friend. They are happy to oblige this request.*

Clementine likes slow circles on their clit and – *Our friend cuts my partner off,* I know, I've done my research. *We all laugh at this.*

I think about this moment, in which the specificity of my desire is important information, information that we are all so happy to communicate about, information that we hold as valuable and necessary. I think about how I hated receiving head for years and years, how I was so dissociated from my body and unable to feel anything when someone went down on me. I think about how the focus on my own pleasure was repulsive to me.

Now my friend moves between my legs, prepared with knowledge of my specific tastes, knowledge that I was able to communicate to them directly. Here in this moment, I am happy, I am at peace.

The sex unfolds between the three of us, it builds in its own rhythms and momentum. I am being smacked and fucked, held and kissed all at once. I am in a tangle of limbs.

I watch the face of our friend as they watch me flying through sub space. There is tenderness and fascination on their face, like they are beholding something both sweet and sacred.

They kiss me between my cries as I move through pain and pleasure. They hold me in their arms while my partner fucks me, hitting me repeatedly.

I rub my own clit in frantic circles, cumming.

References

Anonymous. (2011). *Alcoholics Anonymous: The story of how many thousands of men and women have recovered from alcoholism* (4th ed.). New York, NY: Alcoholics Anonymous World Services, Inc.

Ballard, L.-M. (1991). Fairies and the supernatural on Reachrai. In P. Narváez (Ed.), *The Good People: New fairylore essays*. Bolder, CO: The University of Kentucky Press.

Barad, K. (2011). Nature's queer performativity. *Qui parle: Critical Humanities and Social Sciences*, 19(2).

Ben-Moshe, L. (2014). Alternatives to (disability) incarceration. In L.Ben-Moshe, C. Chapman, & A. Carey (Eds.). *Disability incarcerated: Imprisonment and disability in the United States and Canada* (pp. 255-272). New York: Palgrave MacMillan.

Berne, P. (2015). Disability justice – a working draft. *Sins invalid: An unashamed claim to beauty in the face of invisibility*. Retrieved from http://sinsinvalid.org/blog/disability-justice-a-working-draft-by-patty-berne

Butler, G. R. (1991). The lutin tradition in French-Newfoundland culture: Discourse and belief. In P. Narváez (Ed.), *The Good People: New fairylore essays*. Bolder, CO: The University Press of Kentucky.

Chen, M. (2012). *Animacies: Biopolitics, racial mattering and queer affect*.Durham, NC: Duke University Press.

Clare, E. (2012). Meditations on natural worlds, disabled bodies, and a politics of cure. *Disability studies initiative: University of Wisconsin – Madison*. Retrieved from http://disabilitystudies.wisc.edu/wp-content/uploads/2012/09/Eli-Clare-Meditations-UW-Madison.pdf

Cresswell, M. (2005). Psychiatric "survivors" and testimonies of self-harm. *Social science & medicine*, 61(8), 1668-1677.

Cunneen, S. (1999). Breaking Mary's silence: A feminist reflection on Marian piety. *Theology Today*, 56(3).

Davis, A. Y. (2011). *Are Prisons Obsolete?* New York: Seven Stories Press.

Diamond, S. (2013). What makes us a community? In B. A. LeFrançois, R. Menzies & G. Reaume (Eds.). *Mad Matters: A critical reader in Canadian Mad Studies* (pp. 64-78). Toronto: Canadian Scholar's Press.

de Haardt, M. (2011). The Marian Paradox: Marian practices as a road to a new Mariology? *Feminist Theology*, 19(2).

Edelman, L. (2004). *No future: Queer theory and the death drive*. Durham, NC: Duke University Press.

Erevelles, N. (2011). *Disability and difference in global contexts: Enabling a transformative body politic*. New York, NY: Palgrave Macmillan.

Fabris, E. & K. Aubrecht. Chemical constraint: Experiences of psychiatric coercion, restraint, and detention as carceratory techniques. In L. Ben-Moshe, C. Chapman, & A. Carey (Eds.). *Disability Incarcerated: Imprisonment and Disability in the United States and Canada* (pp. 185-200). New York: Palgrave MacMillan

Federici, S. (2004). *Caliban and the witch: Women, the body and primitive accumulation*. New York, NY: Autonomedia.

Hand, W. (1981). European fairy lore in the New World. *Folklore*, 92(2).

Ingram, G.B., Bouthillette, A., & Retter, Y. (1997). Narratives of place: Subjective and collective. *Queers in space: Communities, public places, sites of resistance* (55-61). Bay Press.

Jenkins, R. P. (1991). Witches and fairies: Supernatural aggression and deviance among the Irish peasantry. In P. Narváez (Ed.), *The Good People: New fairylore essays*. Bolder, CO: The University Press of Kentucky.

Jung, C. G. (2011). *Synchronicity: An acausal connecting principle* (4th ed.). Princeton, NJ: Princeton University Press.

Kafer, A. (2013). *Feminist, queer, crip*. Bloomington, IN: Indiana University Press.

Kieckhefer, R. (2014). *Magic in the Middle Ages* (2nd ed.). (n.p.): Cambridge University Press.

Kimmerer, R. W. (2013). *Braiding sweetgrass: Indigenous wisdom, scientific knowledge and the teachings of plants*. Portland, ME: Milkweed Editions

Kors, A. C., & Peters, E. (Eds.). (2000). *Witchcraft in Europe, 400-1700: A documentary history* (2nd ed.). Philadelphia, PA: University of Pennsylvania Press.

LaViolette, P., & Mcintosh, A. (1997). Fairy hills: merging heritage and conservation. *Ecos*, 18(3/4).

Lysaght, P. (1991). Fairylore from the Midlands of Ireland. In P. Narváez (Ed.), *The Good People: New fairylore essays*. Bolder, CO: The University of Kentucky Press.

Mbembe, A. (2008). Necropolitics. In Morton, S., & Bygrave, S. (Eds.), *Foucault in an age of terror*. (n.p.): Palgrave Macmillan.

McGraw, E. J. (1996). *The moorchild*. (n.p.): Margaret K. McElderry Books.

McRuer, R. (2006). *Crip theory: Cultural signs of queerness and disability*. New York, NY: New York University Press.

Million, D. (2013). *Therapeutic nations: Healing in an age of Indigenous human rights*. Tucson, AZ: University of Arizona.

Mingus, M. (2011). Moving toward the ugly: A politic beyond desirability. *Leaving Evidence*. Retrieved from http://leavingevidence.wordpress.com/2011/08/22/ moving-toward-the-ugly-a-politic-beyond-desirability

Morrigan, C. & geoff (2015). Deconstructing intoxication culture: Community, accessibility and sober spaces.

Mortimer-Sandilands, C., & Erikson, B. (Eds.). (2010). *Queer ecologies: Sex,nature, politics, desire*. Bloomington, IN: Indiana University Press.

Muñoz, J. E. (2009). *Cruising utopia: The then and there of queer futurity*, NewYork, NY: NYU Press.

Narváez, P. Newfoundland berry pickers 'in the fairies.' In P. Narváez (Ed.), *The Good People: New fairylore essays*. Bolder, CO: The University of Kentucky Press.

Ndopu, E. (2014). Don't deny me my disability, dignity, and equal opportunity. *Mail & guardian: Africa's best read*. Retrieved from http://mg.co.za/ article/2014-11-21-dont-deny-me-my-disability-dignity-and-equal opportunity

Neilsen, L. (2008). Lyric inquiry. In Knowles, G. J., & Cole, A. L. (Eds.), *Handbook of the arts in qualitative research*. (n.p.): Sage.

Nelson, K. (2015). Gaslighting is a common victim-blaming bbuse tactic – Here are 4 ways to recognize it in your life. *Everyday Feminism*. Retrieved from http:// everydayfeminism.com/2015/06/gaslighting-is-an-abuse-tactic/

Ó Giolláin, D. (1991). The fairy belief and official religion in Ireland. In Narváez, P. (Ed.), *The Good People: New fairylore essays*. Bolder, CO: The University of Kentucky Press.

Piepzna-Samarasinha, L. L. (2015). *Bodymaps*. Toronto, ON: Mawenzi House Publishers Ltd.

Piepzna-Samarasinha, L. L. (2015). *Dirty river: A queer femme of color dreaming her way home*. Vancouver: Arsenal Pulp Press.

Price, M. (2015). The bodymind problem and the possibilities of pain. *Hypatia* 30(1).

Razack, S. (2002). When place becomes race. *Race, space and the law: Unmapping a white settler society* (1-20). Toronto: Between the Lines.

Reavey, P., & Brown, S. D. (2006) Transforming past agency and action in thepresent time, social remembering and child sexual abuse. *Theory & Psychology* 16(2).

Riotfag, N. (2010). *Towards a less fucked up world: Sobriety and anarchist struggle.* (n.p.): Riotfag, N.

Samuels, E. (2011). Cripping anti-futurity, or, if you love queer theory so much, why don't you marry it? *Disability Studies quarterly* 3.

Scott, S. (2015). *witchbody*. Chicago, IL: Perfectly Acceptable Press.

Shakespeare, T. (2006). The social model of disability. In Davis, L. J. (Ed.), *Disability studies reader.* (n.p.): Taylor & Francis.

Shimrat, I. (2013). The tragic farce of "community mental healthcare." In B. A. LeFrançois, R. Menzies & G. Reaume (Eds.). *Mad Matters: A critical reader in Canadian Mad Studies* (pp. 144-157). Toronto: Canadian Scholar's Press.

Simpson, L. B. (2016). Not murdered, not missing. *Leannesimpson.ca.* Retrieved from http://www.leannesimpson.ca/writings/not-murdered-not-missing-re belling-against-colonial-gender-violence

Spell. (2017). *In Merriam-Webster.com.* Retrieved from http://www.merriam-webster.com/ dictionary/spell

Stolorow, R. D. (2016). Trauma and temporality. *Psychoanalytic Psychology* 20(1).

Taylder, S. (2004). Our lady of the libido: Towards a Marian Theology of sexual liberation? *Feminist Theology*, 12(3).

Vander Kolk , B. A. (2015). The body keeps the score: Brain, mind, and body in the healing of trauma. Penguin Books.

Ware, S, J. Ruzsa & G. Dias. It can't be fixed because it's not broken: Racism and disability in the Prison Industrial Complex. In In L. Ben-Moshe, C. Chapman, & A. Carey (Eds.). *Disability incarcerated: Imprisonment and Disability in the United States and Canada* (pp. 163-184). New York: Palgrave MacMillan.

Wintemberg , K. H., & Wintemberg , W. J. (1918). Folk-lore from Grey County, Ontario. *The journal of American folklore, 31.*

Youthdale Treatment Centres. (n.d.) Secure treatment to help children in a safe environment. *Youthdale.* Retrieved from http://youthdale.ca/en/crisis _services/ secure_treatment_unit.php

Acknowledgements

A version of *Intoxication Spaces: Mental Maps of Substance Use* first appeared in the Spring 2016 issue of *Peak Magazine*. It is reprinted here with permission.

A version of *Trauma Time: The Queer Temporalities of the Traumatized Mind* first appeared in *Somatechnics 7(1)*. It is reprinted here with permission.

A version of *Failure to Comply: Madness and/as Testimony* first appeared in *Canadian Journal of Disability Studies, 6(3)*. It is reprinted here with permission.

A version of *Fucking Crazy: On Complex Trauma, Surviving Sexual Violence, and Living My Best Slut Life* first appeared in *Hamilton Arts & Letters, 12(1)*. It is reprinted here with permission.

I would like to thank my friends and fellow students during my Masters degree who thought through many of these ideas with me. I would like to thank my supervisor Nancy Halifax for her support and encouragement.

Thank you to Tara McGowan-Ross for her incredible editing skills and breathing new life into this book.

Thank you to Devan Murphy for the beautiful cover.

Thank you to my partner Jay, for having my back, and being by my side as I koolaide man into the next dimension.

About the Writer

Clementine Morrigan is a writer. She is the writer behind the zine series *Fucking Magic*, and the zines *Love Without Emergency, Fuck the Police Means We Don't Act Like Cops to Each Other, Fucking Crazy*, and *Fucking Girls*. They also wrote the books *You Can't Own the Fucking Stars, The Size of a Bird*, and *Rupture*. Two more books are forthcoming, *Sexting*, and *Fucking Magic*. She has been writing and publishing for more than 20 years and has many more projects on the way. They are also a podcaster as one half of the podcast *Fucking Cancelled* and the creator the popular *Trauma Informed Polyamory* workshop. She teaches other online workshops like *Bisexual Girls with Baggage* and *Disorganized Attachment Is a Fucking Trip*. They are an ecosocialist, an anarchist, an abolitionist, an opposer of cancel culture, a trauma educator, a sex educator, a person living with complex ptsd, a sober alcoholic, a polyamorous bisexual dyke, and a proud dog mom to Clover "the dog" Morrigan. Find more of her work at clementinemorrigan. com.

CPSIA information can be obtained
at www.ICGtesting.com
Printed in the USA
BVHW081350290821
615167BV00006B/16